CHARTING YOUR DESTINY

Riding on the Wings of a Father

David S. Philemon

Royal Diadem Publishing Inc.

To the Almighty God, my Rock, Refuge, and Source of all wisdom and strength. Thank You for Your unwavering love, grace, and the purpose You've placed within me. May this book bring glory to Your name and draw others closer to You.

And to my beloved spiritual parents, Dr. Paul and Dr. Mrs. Becky Paul Enenche, who have faithfully nurtured and guided me in this journey. Your example of unwavering devotion, godly counsel, and compassionate care has been a beacon of light and strength in my life. Thank you for standing as pillars of faith and for your steadfast commitment to the Kingdom.

ACKNOWLEDGEMENT

This book would not have been possible without the unwavering support, dedication, and talent of an extraordinary team. My deepest gratitude goes to each of you for your contributions, insights, and encouragement throughout this journey.

First and foremost, thank you to Rev. Mimi Philemon my dear wife, Rev. Shina Gentry, and and my assistant pastor Rev. Bright Amudoaghan for your incredible effort, encouragement, and belief in this project. Your support has been instrumental in bringing this vision to life.

To the dedicated leaders of Royal Diadem Publishing, Ide Imogie and Kishawna Bailey, I am immensely grateful for your belief in this project from the very beginning and for investing your time and energy into its development. Your creativity, dedication, and expertise have been the backbone of this endeavor.

I am especially grateful to the Royal Diadem Publishing team— Beulah Orogun, Emmanuella Ben-Eboh, Doyinsade Awodele, Kim Matthews, and Shante Gill, for your meticulous attention to detail, refining every page and ensuring that each word reflects our vision.

A heartfelt thank you to my family, friends, and colleagues whose unwavering support and belief in this project gave me the courage and strength to see it through.

Finally, thank you to all the readers and supporters who make this work meaningful. I am humbled and honored to share this journey with each of you.

With all my gratitude,
David Philemon

CONTENTS

INTRODUCTION

God, in his loving and fatherly nature, has never intended for us to walk through life struggling, fumbling, or unthinkingly making mistakes because we are unsure of whether the principles we apply are correct. Life is too short for endless experimenting and hoping you are on the right path. No, no, no! God's intention has always been clear: His heart desires that you rise high in life by riding on the shoulders of spiritual fathers, men and women whose lives have been molded by experience, wisdom, and divine guidance. God's ultimate desire is to usher you into a glorious destiny through them. Pause momentarily and think: what would you see when you observe people struggling endlessly, battling through life without direction? It is often because they have neglected this fundamental spiritual principle of submission to a spiritual father.

In life, we can learn through painful experiences or through the guidance of those who have already traveled our path. Yes, that's a powerful truth! The journey of destiny is not a journey we are meant to travel alone, and God, in His infinite wisdom, has set up a system where spiritual fathers act as guides, mentors, and cover for spiritual sons and daughters. Through their wisdom, instruction, and anointing, we can ascend more quickly and safely to the heights God has destined for us.

Come to think of it, why struggle when you can soar? Why make mistakes when you can be guided? Why experiment with your life when you can be sure? If you are truly honest about the answer to these questions, I am sure you are beginning to see the essence for which the Holy Spirit has led you to pick this book. This spiritual father's experiences and guidance are meant to be your map, their prayers are meant for your protection, and their anointing is meant to be the wind beneath your wings. So, child of God, instead of wasting years trying to figure things out, it's time to heed the call of wisdom and submit.

One of the most complex phenomena for many people is "the concept of submission." In the world of today, where many people believe in independence and self-reliance, the idea of submitting to another person sounds distasteful to many, and some even go as far as seeing it as a form of bondage, but in the spiritual realm, submission is not about control; it's about alignment, and it's about recognizing that God has placed certain people in your life to guide you, to protect you, and to help you reach your destiny in flying colors. Are you genuinely set to end the constant struggles of your life? Are you tired of endlessly toiling without results? Then, you must master this principle of submission to a spiritual father.

"Riding on the Wings of a Father" is more than just a book; it's a blueprint for destiny. You will be set for a life of ease and obedience as you read. This is a journey of great transformation and exponential results.

God is about to do great things with you, so let's get into it immediately!

CHAPTER ONE

THE WINGS OF FATHERS

"True transformation begins when you grasp the depth of God's unfailing love and the guidance of a spiritual father."

The Power Of A Father's Hand

Someone Must Make You Submit

"Can a woman forget her sucking child, that she should not have compassion on the son of her womb? yea, they may forget, yet will I not forget thee." (Isaiah 49:15) These words, my beloved, carry a weight of truth that can shake the very foundations of your understanding, they speak of a love so profound, so steadfast that it surpasses even the deepest bonds we know in this earthly realm; yet, as impossible as it may seem, I have witnessed with mine own eyes the tragedy of mothers forsaking their children, turning away from the fruit of their wombs. But hear me well, for even in the face of such heartbreak; our Lord declares a truth most magnificent, that even if a mother could forget her child, He, the Almighty, will never,

ever forget you. This revelation, this truth of God's unfailing love and remembrance, is one you must grasp with every fiber of your being. You must let it seep into the marrow of your bones, for without this anchor, your journey through life will be fraught with unnecessary complications. Why do I say this with such urgency? Because, my dear ones, we find ourselves in a time of great spiritual significance - this is the year of the talking serpent, the year of the biting serpents, and glory to God, the year of the rising gods.

Now, you may furrow your brows at this, wondering what on earth I'm speaking of, but listen closely, for I'm about to unveil a truth that will set your spirit ablaze. You see, you will never truly comprehend the substance of your being, the power that courses through your veins until you face the very thing that was meant to be your demise and emerge victorious. When that which was designed to destroy you crumbles at your feet, defeated, the news will spread like wildfire through the spiritual realm that *"You don't confront this one and live."* Because they are never alone, they have "a Father"; there is God who will never forget them just as a mother never forgets her suckling child, and also they have a spiritual father, a spiritual backing who never forgets them.

This is the revelation I want you to capture and hold fast to in your spirit, so I implore you to stay in the spirit as you keep reading! By the grace of God, I had the incomparable privilege of visiting my father in the Lord as of 2023. In the privacy of his office, within the sanctity of his home, my father laid his hand upon my head, and for full twelve minutes as I knelt before him, the anointing oil flowed, and his hand remained steadfast upon my head. In those moments, mysteries beyond human comprehension unfolded. Even now, anytime I think of it, I still feel the weight of his hand upon my head, I still feel the weight of that blessing upon me; it's as if a mark, not like a tattoo, more like a spiritual keloid, has been etched indelibly into my head, I tell you the truth, the impact of that moment, the transformation it wrought within me, defies all human description.

Through years of ministry and spiritual growth, I have come to understand a fundamental truth, "for anyone to become something of significance, someone must make them," and the identity of the one shaping you is paramount because it determines the trajectory of your life and the essence of what you will become. For example, if you walk into a Motorola store, you cannot expect to purchase an Apple product. Why? Because the Motorola mindset is running the place. Also, when you hold an Apple product in your hands, regardless of your feelings towards the company or its people, do you realize you cannot deny the quality and essence of the product? Why? It bears the unmistakable mark of excellence, attitude, software, and behaviors that come from the specific vision and approach of the Apple company. This means "you are ultimately going to be the product of the man making you, you will have the spirit of your father, the mind of your father, the blessings of your father, et.c." Now, let me take you back to the book of Genesis, where we see a fascinating moment. For the first time in recorded history, God utters a peculiar phrase to the host of Heaven: "Go to!"

Understanding The Journey

And the Lord said, Behold, the people is one, and they have all one language; and this they begin to do: and now nothing will be restrained from them, which they have imagined to do. Go to, let us go down, and there confound their language, that they may not understand one another's speech. (Genesis 11:6-7)

This "Go to!" is a call to action and a divine decree with far-reaching implications. God recognized that as long as humanity's ability to communicate remained unhindered, their capacity to comprehend and achieve would know no bounds. So He said, "Go to! Let us ensure they don't understand each other." Why? Because without clear understanding, there can be no direction; without direction, there can be no distinction.

Think about this moment: it doesn't matter how vast a person's potential may be; if they lack a clear understanding of spiritual matters, they will inevitably lack direction. So when you encounter someone who bears the hallmarks of greatness yet behaves like a defeated soul, do not judge. Instead, look upon them with compassion and declare, "I cast out the spirit of confusion ("Go to") in the name of Jesus!" Multitudes are walking among us who are victims of this divine "Go to!" God said, "Go to! Let's make sure they don't understand." You see, without understanding, there can be no obedience to instructions. Without obedience to instructions, you cannot lay hold of the spiritual transfer and impartation meant to come from a father to you. In other words, you will never partake of anything that could radically transform your life.

Walking with God, my friends is long and arduous; consider the patriarch Abraham; it wasn't until he was 158 years old that God declared, "Now I know." Abraham lived to the ripe old age of 175, did he not? So, at the age of 75, when God first called him, He began a process of testing and proving that lasted nearly six decades. In those days, human lifespans were considerably longer, but in our time, we see people throwing in the towel in their 20s and 30s. So, do you think you have Six decades to fail God's test continually? Not! You will have to hurry and perfect your ways faster, which is why you cannot joke with the place of a father in your life; they can hurry your journey!

The fathers, the spiritual patriarchs, carry within them the ability to lift you up and impart the wisdom and strength you need for the journey ahead. As my father so eloquently said, "Fathers are feathers." They can serve as ladders for you to climb or as wings upon which you can soar. Fathers are spiritual elevators, capable of raising us to heights we could never reach. The choice, ultimately, is yours. The book of Proverbs says, *"There is a way which seemeth right unto a man, but the end thereof are the ways of death."* (Proverbs 14:12). However, there is also a way of the Spirit, a path of divine guidance and supernatural empowerment, this is the way fathers can guide you through, but if you choose to go on your way, you may end up destroying yourself.

In the book of Job, we see an excellent description of this spiritual truth, *"There is a path which no fowl knoweth, and which the vulture's eye hath not seen: The lion's whelps have not trodden it, nor the fierce lion passed by it."* (Job 28:7-8) This is a realm where natural laws and human understanding fall short, and God's power manifests in ways that defy our limited comprehension. The passage continues, *"He putteth forth his hand upon the rock; he overturneth the mountains by the roots."* (Job 28:9). How can the mere act of laying hands upon a rock result in overturning mountains? This, my friends, is the mystery and power of spiritual impartation. Perhaps you face a problem in your life that looms before you like an insurmountable mountain; instead of exhausting yourself trying to scale it through your efforts, learn to submit to Fathers and let them lay hands upon the root of the problem through prayer and faith, then watch as God turns that mountain upside down before your very eyes. This is the way of the Spirit, the hidden path that even the keenest natural senses cannot understand.

While your peers and colleagues are striving to overcome seemingly impossible situations, you have the opportunity to walk into a different reality by discovering and walking in this hidden path of the Spirit: to submit to fathers who have gone ahead and allowed their hands to guide you. Through this, you can navigate life's challenges with supernatural ease and effectiveness that will leave others in awe.

Job 28:10 says, *"He cutteth out rivers among the rocks, and his eye seeth every precious thing."* This means that when you walk in the Spirit by submitting to fathers, you won't miss the opportunities God places before you; where others see only hardship and impossibility, your spiritually attuned eyes will perceive the potential for living waters to flow. That rock that appears to others as an immovable obstacle will become a source of life-giving waters for you. This was the reality of the children of Israel because they had a father called Moses.

To violate or ignore this spiritual path always comes at a cost. You have two options: "You either learn from the experiences of others (fathers) or through your painful trials." But be warned, learning solely from your own experiences can exact such a heavy toll that you may not be able to pay the price in a single lifetime. However, when you humble yourself to learn from the experiences of others, or better yet, receive impartation from a vessel of higher spiritual caliber, your life's journey becomes smoother and more abundantly blessed.

Some proudly say, *"I want to learn from my own experiences."* But I ask you, why would you choose to pay such a heavy price when you can benefit from the hard-earned wisdom of those who have gone before you? This is the wisdom of spiritual transfer, the process of spiritual selection. Do you know a man and woman can come together without any thought or intention, simply allowing nature to take its course, and they will give birth to a male or female child? But there is also a more deliberate and even scientific approach, where they can choose the optimal time for conception, make the proper deposits at the right moment, and then have the desired sex of the child that they want.

If they use the first approach, it doesn't matter how much they desire to have a girl; they may keep coming up with boys. Still, suppose they follow the scientific approach, likened to the approach of following fathers with knowledge and experience. In that case, they can better determine their outcome when coming together. What I am saying is if you want to be deliberate about your life and want to be great, you must be intentional about submitting to your father's guidance so that the outcome of your life will be nothing short of greatness.

Oh, I pray you do not miss the depth of what I just shared!

Wisdom And Instructions

Just as in the natural realm, where science can make it possible to influence the gender of a child, in the spiritual realm, we have always had the power of selection through faith and prayer. This means you have the right and the responsibility to be intentional about what you receive and what you allow to take root in your life. You can look at your life and say, "I have acquired this much wisdom, but I need more understanding in this area." Or, "I have grown in patience, but I need to develop more boldness." Or perhaps, "I haven't yet cultivated the fruits of the Spirit; I need to grow in love, joy, peace, longsuffering, gentleness, goodness, faith, meekness, and temperance." You can choose the spiritual attributes and gifts you wish to cultivate.

This process of spiritual selection means you have a role to play in your spiritual growth; you can observe, discern, and decide, "I want to develop this virtue, that gift, and this aspect of godly character." Although modern science is only now grappling with the concept of selection in the natural realm, the people of God have been practicing this in the spiritual realm for millennia. There is a path in the spirit that science is only now beginning to comprehend, and while researchers labor to understand the intricacies of genetics and heredity, there was a woman in Scripture who didn't need a doctor's expertise; she only needed a priest's anointing (her spiritual father's anointing).

This woman, Hannah, looked at her circumstances and said to the Lord, "Lord, I see the blessings of children all around me, and children are indeed a blessing. But I see something different in my life. I see a priest, I see a prophet, I see a king. That's the one I want. If You give me that man-child, I will return him to You." And Eli the priest, discerning the fervor of her silent prayer, proclaimed, *"Go in peace: and the God of Israel grant thee thy petition that thou hast asked of him."* (1 Samuel 1:17) Hannah departed, her heart at peace, and the Lord remembered her. When next Elkanah knew his wife, she conceived. Upon the birth of her son, Hannah testified, "For this child I prayed; and the Lord hath given me my petition which I asked of him." (1 Samuel 1:27). This is the same thing she had been praying to get for years, and it didn't come, but the moment her father spoke and instructed her to go that her request would be granted, it was done! See, no matter what you do, never neglect your father's place and his instructions! You will miss great blessings in your life if you do!

Instructions from People's Experiences

If someone has experienced failure, I can glean the lessons from their missteps, understand the reasons behind their downfall, and add that knowledge to my repository of wisdom, revelation, and instruction. As Solomon, in his God-given wisdom, said, *"I went by the field of the slothful, and by the vineyard of the man void of understanding; And, lo, it was all grown over with thorns, and nettles had covered the face thereof, and the stone wall thereof was broken down. Then I saw and considered it well: I looked upon it and received instruction."* (Proverbs 24:30-32)

Do you see what he said? "The foolishness of a lazy man instructed me." This means Solomon could learn from the man's field that the lazy man's problem wasn't the field itself but his mindset. Solomon realized that this lazy man could lament and rage over his financial circumstances or poverty life as much as he wanted, but it would never change anything as long as he was lazy. This means Solomon didn't need to be lazy to find out what would happen if he was lazy; he was already learning from this man's experience; let us look at the passion translation. Solomon declared, *"When I looked, I saw and considered it well. I received instruction."* The Passion Translation renders it as "I received instructions." Solomon intentionally observed the field of the slothful man so that he could select valuable lessons from that experience.

Do you see the profound truth here? I don't have to personally experience every pitfall and setback to learn from them. I can learn vicariously through the experiences of others, I can choose which lessons I want to internalize, and I don't have to wait for failure to be my teacher. I can learn from both the successes and failures of those who have gone before me, particularly from spiritual fathers who have walked the path of faith longer than I have.

Let me share a poignant example from Scripture. Abraham, the father of faith, thought it wise to journey to Egypt when famine struck the land of promise; despite God's assurance of blessing, Abraham felt compelled to seek his solution, so he ventured into Egypt, found sustenance, but returned with more than he bargained for, he came back with Hagar and from Hagar came Ishmael as a consequence that reverberates through history even to this day. Years later, Isaac, Abraham's son, was on the brink of repeating his father's mistake because, in Genesis 26, another famine descended upon the land. Isaac's first instinct was to follow in his father's footsteps and to go down to Egypt in search of provision, but God intervened, saying, *"Go not down into Egypt; dwell in the land which I shall tell thee of."* (Genesis 26:2) God reminded Isaac of the covenant, god was warning him, "Hey boy, if you descend into Egypt as your father did, you will create your own set of problems. Remember Hagar? Remember Ishmael? One Ishmael was more than enough."

God was, in effect, telling Isaac that if he chose to go to Egypt, he would have to learn the hard way through bitter experience. "Your father waited 25 years to have you. Now look at your situation - your wife is also barren. But don't make the mistake of trying to solve this dilemma through your own devices." When Isaac faced barrenness, just as his father had, he could have quickly resorted to the same flawed solution, but he didn't. Also, when he faced famine, he could have resorted to the same flawed decision of picking a maid, but again, He didn't because God said, no, remain where I tell you, and put your trust in Me. Had Isaac gone to Egypt, he might have acquired his own "Hagar," bringing further complications into the family line.

Instead, what did Isaac do? He entreated the Lord on behalf of his wife, Rebekah. He prayed, and God opened her womb. It wasn't Abraham's prayers or any action of Abraham that brought forth children to Isaac. Isaac approached God and interceded for his wife; the solution came through fervent prayer, not through a hasty shortcut. He had learned from His father, Abraham, that going to Egypt to find food or get another lady to produce children was wrong. This was wisdom and instruction from the experience of a father. So, who is your father, and what are you learning from his experiences today?

God had revealed to Isaac the power of faith and patience, not quick fixes or human strategies, all through his father's life, Abraham. Sometimes, when there is barrenness in your life, be it physical, financial, spiritual, or relational, you may be tempted to seek an alternative route, a shortcut to your desired outcome. However, alternatives can lead to long-term problems and consequences that may echo through generations; the barrenness you face might not be solely physical; there can be financial drought, spiritual stagnation, or relational discord. Nevertheless, I want you to know that the solution isn't always the quickest or most prominent. Look at the fathers who have gone before you; reach out to them, and you will receive wisdom and instructions regarding your situation.

Now, Watch This Closely:

Even after 20 long years of barrenness in their marriage, Isaac and Rebekah's breakthrough came because Isaac prayed and trusted God's perfect timing. Right now, you are reading this, and you may be facing situations where you've been waiting, and waiting, and waiting some more. You are probably sorely tempted to take matters into your own hands, to seek out shortcuts that promise quick relief, but I stand before you today to decree and declare that this, right here and now, is your season of breakthrough!

You may have been wrestling with doubts and wondering if serving God, obeying His commandments, and honoring His name was all in vain; the enemy may have whispered in your ear, "Is God listening? Is this walk of faith even worth the trouble?" But let me tell you something, child of God, and I want you to let this truth sink deep into your spirit: God is not a scam! I'll repeat it: God is not a scam! The Bible says, "They looked unto him, and were lightened: and their faces were not ashamed." (Psalm 34:5). Now, hear me well, those who deal crookedly with God, who try to manipulate His promises or twist His Word for their gain, they indeed end up suffering the consequences of their actions. But God never fails those who walk in faithfulness before Him; I often use my own life as an example, putting myself and my family at risk of misunderstanding or even ridicule, but I care not for the opinions of men - if just one wise soul can glean wisdom from our testimony, then it's all worth it. Instead of walking in confusion and trying to be a Superman, it's time to talk to a father!

Let me share with you a powerful testimony from my own family. There was a time when they had absolutely nothing - and when I say nothing, they were scraping the bottom of the barrel. My heart was heavy for their situation, so I called them to join me in a three-day night vigil. We sought the face of God together, crying out for His intervention. During that time of intense prayer, God granted me a vision, and I saw an airplane flying overhead. I didn't fully understand the significance of this vision at the time, but I knew in my spirit that it was a sign of something big on the horizon. So I shared with them, "I see an airplane flying. I don't know exactly what it means, but I can tell you something big is coming your way."

Two weeks after this prophetic word, my sister, who had studied mass communication but had always harbored a passion for cooking as a hobby, she received a life-changing contract.

A significant airline known worldwide for its quality service had made a grave error with its in-flight meal service. An insect was found in one of the meals, causing the airline's management to panic. Their reputation for impeccable food quality was at stake, and they were at a loss for what to do. God's plan began to unfold in this moment of crisis.

A woman familiar with my sister's culinary skills suddenly remembered, "I know someone who can cook!" Without hesitation, she reached out to my sister with this unexpected opportunity. Do you see how prophecy connects the dots in ways we could never anticipate? Bless her heart, my sister didn't start quibbling about payment or contracts right away. No, she recognized this for what it was: a divine opportunity. Her eyes were open to see the precious thing God had placed before her, just as Job 28:10 declares, *"His eye seeth every precious thing."*

My sister's spiritual eyes were tuned to recognize opportunities, and she stepped boldly into the moment God had prepared for her. She demonstrated flexibility, readiness to deliver, and a willingness to serve, all qualities that position us to receive God's blessings. This was how her story changed completely.

Many people find themselves in similar situations right now; opportunities are hovering all around them, but their spiritual eyes must be opened to perceive them; this is why you need a father over you. Sometimes, the opportunity will align perfectly with your field of expertise; other times, it will come from an unexpected direction outside your comfort zone. But I declare today, in the name of Jesus, that something big is coming your way, and your eyes will be opened to see it, your heart will be prepared to receive it, and you will walk in the fullness of God's plans for your life!

The Power Of Spiritual Lineage

You see, this is a great truth that many in the body of Christ have yet to understand fully; the power of spiritual lineage is never something to overlook. Just as we inherit certain traits and tendencies from our natural parents, we also receive spiritual DNA from our spiritual fathers. In 2 Kings 2, we have a powerful illustration of this principle in the life of Elisha, the servant of Elijah. He understood the importance of spiritual impartation and transfers, so as Elijah's time on earth drew close, Elisha refused to leave his side. When Elijah asked what he desired, Elisha boldly requested, *"I pray thee, let a double portion of thy spirit be upon me."* (2 Kings 2:9)

Now, you may think, "How presumptuous of Elisha to ask for such a thing!" But I tell you, Elisha understood something crucial about the kingdom of God. He knew that the kingdom operates on the principle of impartation and inheritance from a father, and he knew that to carry on Elijah's ministry, he needed more than just knowledge or skill; he needed the very spirit that empowered Elijah's miraculous works.

Elijah then said, *"Thou hast a hard thing: nevertheless, if thou see me when I am taken from thee, it shall be so unto thee; but if not, it shall not be so."* (2 Kings 2:10). This transfer of spiritual power required Elisha's unwavering focus and determination, he had to be spiritually attuned with his spiritual eyes wide open and ready to receive this impartation. And we know the rest of the story, Elisha did indeed see Elijah taken up in a whirlwind, and he received that double portion. The evidence of this impartation was evident in his ministry; Elisha performed twice as many recorded miracles as his spiritual father, Elijah.

This, my friends, is the power of spiritual fatherhood and impartation; it's not just about learning principles or memorizing scriptures, though these things are essential. It's about receiving a spiritual mantle, an anointing that empowers you to operate in a realm beyond your natural abilities.

Now, I can almost hear you thinking, "But what if I don't have a spiritual father? What if I haven't found someone to teach me this way?" Take heart, beloved. While having a physical, spiritual father is a tremendous blessing, our ultimate Father is God. As

Jesus declared, *"Call no man your father upon the earth: for one is your Father, which is in heaven."* (Matthew 23:9). This doesn't negate the role of spiritual fathers in the earthly realm. Still, it reminds us that all true spiritual impartation comes from God. However, you need to ask God to open your eyes; there is a Father He has ordained to guide you because God always delights in using human vessels to transmit His power and anointing to us. If you find yourself without a spiritual father in the natural, press into God with all your might, seek His face with the same tenacity that Elisha showed, and declare, like Jacob, "I will not let thee go, except thou bless me." (Genesis 32:26). Through all these two things will happen. First, God will begin to bless you; secondly, he will direct you on whom to submit.

I declare over you now, may your spiritual eyes be opened, and may you see every precious thing God places before you. May you walk in the fullness of your spiritual inheritance, operating in human wisdom and the power of God's Spirit as he guides you on who to submit to in the name of Jesus.

CHAPTER TWO

TAKE CAUTION!

"A spiritual father is not just a guide but a living vessel of faith, prosperity, and wisdom; honor him, and you will flourish."

The Peril Of Familiarity

There's a dangerous pitfall many believers keep stumbling into: the trivialization of spiritual fathers due to familiarity. This mindset is a root cause of struggle for countless souls who fail to learn from the experiences and wisdom of those God has placed over them. It matters not how close you may be to a prophet or a man of God; your foolishness and disobedience can never be overridden by mere prophetic connection because your obedience plays a pivotal role in validating that connection. Otherwise, you can find yourself in the peculiar position of being near a prophet and still suffering like a pauper simply because you rely on your understanding rather than heeding the wisdom of your spiritual father.

Proverbs 3:5-6 (KJV) says, *"Trust in the Lord with all thine heart, and lean not unto thine own understanding. In all thy ways acknowledge him, and he shall direct thy paths."* This scripture shows us the importance of trusting in God's wisdom. I need you to know that this wisdom often comes through the vessel of our spiritual fathers rather than relying solely on our limited understanding. I still recall a critical moment when my father said, "Wow, you traveled all this way just to bring your first fruit offering?" He was happy at my obedience and reverence for him, and you know what? Many sons fail to benefit from their patriarchal relationship because they don't know how to be sons. They lack the humility and discernment to recognize the example set before them and to follow it with devotion and obedience.

God has raised spiritual fathers to be examples of faith, obedience, and prosperity in the Kingdom. Look at 1 Corinthians 4:15 (KJV) says, *"For though ye have ten thousand instructors in Christ, yet have ye not many fathers: for in Christ Jesus I have begotten you through the gospel."* Do you get it? This shows us true spiritual fathers' rare nature and importance in our walk with Christ.

The Power of Obedience and Trust

When we talk about serving God the right way, I implore you to learn from those of us who are passionately serving Him. "When a man gives you water from the rock, don't ever fear to trust. Even if the bottled water he holds cannot satisfy you, he will create a rock and provide you with more water." This is the essence of faith and obedience to spiritual authority.

Are you following me? Some say, "The Lord will give you water," but what happens when that water runs out? I'm talking about those who can stand before you and say, "Here, with my hands, the Lord will give you water," then, miraculously, water shows up! This is the power of a true spiritual father, who doesn't just speak of blessings but demonstrates the power of God in tangible ways. If he says, "Don't be afraid," then trust that as long as you are with him, you have nothing to fear, will never run dry, and will always be protected. Truthfully, this level of faith and trust in your spiritual father can open the floodgates of heaven's blessings in your life. In Exodus 17:6 (KJV), the Bible says, *"Behold, I will stand before thee there upon the rock in Horeb; and thou shalt smite the rock, and there shall come water out of it, that the people may drink. And Moses did so in the sight of the elders of Israel."* This miraculous provision of water from the rock is a powerful metaphor for the blessings flowing from obedience to spiritual authority.

I'm sharing this because the same spirit that came upon me from my father has led me to realize that there is a weighty greatness that God wants to bring upon people to take them from nothing and turn them into something extraordinary! However, we must all begin to recognize the place of fathers. This reminds me of the prophecy in Isaiah 60:22 (KJV), *"A little one shall become a thousand, and a small one a strong nation: I the Lord will hasten it in his time."* God is ready to multiply your influence and impact, but it requires your obedience and trust in the spiritual authority He has placed over you.

The Right Mentorship Is The Key To Greatness

I said earlier that someone has made every man who becomes excellent. This is a lesson I've learned from my father, and it's a truth that echoes throughout scripture and history. To become anything significant, you need the right mentorship. Whoever shapes you will influence your path. If a small-minded person makes you, you will remain small. But if a wise, sophisticated spirit shapes you, you will rise to higher places. There are paths that even the eagle's eyes have not seen, and it's through the right mentorship that these paths are revealed to us. Proverbs 13:20 (KJV) says it this way, *"He that walketh with wise men shall be wise: but a companion of fools shall be destroyed."* Choosing the right mentors and spiritual fathers in our journey to greatness is essential.

If you live your life trying to please people at the expense of your spiritual father's instructions, you may eventually lose God's presence, favor, and power; you will even become spiritually dry and lose the very covering meant to protect you. This is a common pitfall that many fall into, often without realizing the gravity of their actions. Look at the example of Saul in the Bible; he initially obeyed God through Samuel the prophet but later grew so proud that he began to disobey his spiritual cover, Samuel. His disobedience of Samuel is what ultimately led to his downfall. Look at this: 1 Samuel 15:22-23 (KJV), *"And Samuel said, Hath the Lord as great delight in burnt offerings and sacrifices, as in obeying the voice of the Lord? Behold, to obey is better than sacrifice, and to hearken than the fat of rams. For rebellion is as the sin of witchcraft, and stubbornness is as iniquity and idolatry. Because thou hast rejected the word of the Lord, he hath also rejected thee from being king."*

Did everyone who walked closely with God have a unique name for Him? For example, Abraham called the place where God provided a ram from him instead of sacrificing Isaac "Jehovah Jireh." "Jehovah Jirel translates to "on the mountain of the Lord it shall be seen, or it shall be found." So when you sacrifice for the Lord, you will find more than you ever sought. He took his only son, whom he loved dearly, and laid him on the altar. At that moment, when he demonstrated his faith, God showed up. This level of intimacy with God often comes through obedience to and reverence for the spiritual fathers He has placed in our lives; I say this because there are many times your spiritual father may instruct you to give a dangerous sacrifice that will touch your heart, I encourage you that you should not rebel on such instruction because more often than not, those instructions are the gates of destiny and tremendous breakthrough you can never imagine

Because of Abraham's obedience, we can all be called children of God today, meaning we all serve God based on one man's encounter. It can be the same with you; if you heed my words, your life, your story, and the generations yet unborn will testify to your success. The world will want to know the secrets of your achievements, and you will give God names that the world will remember. Psalm 9:10 (KJV) says, *"And they that know thy name will put their trust in thee: for thou, Lord, hast not forsaken them that seek thee."* Knowing God intimately, often through the guidance of our spiritual fathers, leads to a deeper trust in Him and His unfailing provision.

In his wisdom, Solomon says if a man ignores his destiny, his destiny will turn against him. This is a deeper dimension of the scripture we read earlier, *"I passed by the field of the slothful and by the vineyard of the man void of understanding; And, lo, it was all grown over with thorns, and nettles had covered the face thereof, and the stone wall thereof was broken down"* (Proverbs 24:30-31, KJV). The lazy person's field reflects neglect, a place filled with excuses for not honoring God and aligning with His will. If you seek wisdom through experience alone, be prepared for thorns, weeds, and broken walls. However, realize that after learning these lessons, you might be too old to benefit from them. Your failures, pain, and shame may become wisdom for the next generation, but this will not be your portion. And I know you will be wise enough to seek the right mentorship.

Be Aggressive In Confidence About Destiny

The Power Of Spiritual Endorsement

Don't sit down waiting for someone to open doors for you. If your father has endorsed and confirmed you, your destiny is open, and it's your responsibility to create opportunities for you. Whether you find resources in your home or the field, seize the moment. Do you remember the story of Jacob? When Esau returned from hunting, Jacob prepared the meal and received blessings. This is how many people are procrastinating their greatness, and as a result, businesses that should have taken off are stuck; you face little resistance, and instead of pushing through, you back down. Are you too lazy to research and make the right moves? This creates an atmosphere of thorns and broken walls around you.

What am I saying? I am saying, if just in the short time it took to get the meal ready, Esau lost the blessings, then I want you to know you don't need to waste any time in pursuing destiny anymore; the fact that God has blessed you through the words and endorsement of your spiritual father is enough for you to walk through destiny with confidence and determination, don't waste time in starting that business, take it with confidence if your spiritual father has spoken; don't waste time in going to school if your spiritual father has spoken; and don't waste time in taking your destiny seriously if your spiritual father has prophesied... His endorsement releases the power of God on your life and endeavors, so be confident as you take destiny aggressively.

One lesson I learned from my Spiritual fathers, and I am saying the same to you as a spiritual father, is, "When you enter a new environment, whether it's Houston, California, or anywhere else, don't sit idle for a week before making an impact. If you want to succeed, start reaching out and making connections immediately." Don't allow anything God has placed in your care to deteriorate or disintegrate; be proactive and take action. As long as a father has blessed you before going, I say to you, take the land.

This reminds us of the instruction given to Joshua in Joshua 1:9 (KJV), *"Have not I commanded thee? Be strong and of good courage; be not afraid, neither be thou dismayed: for the Lord thy God is with thee whithersoever thou goest."* With your spiritual father's blessings, you have heaven's backing, so move forward boldly and confidently toward everything concerning your destiny.

You must adopt an aggressive approach in pursuing and capturing your destiny; if you don't, you will constantly focus on others' shortcomings, wondering who is wrong or who is at fault. Many people know how to run a church better than the senior pastor, but they do it with their mouths; the moment you finally give them the role of a leader, they often find themselves overwhelmed, stressed, and dealing with high blood pressure and various health complications, simply from the pressures of leadership.

Proverbs 29:18 (KJV), *"Where there is no vision, the people perish: but he that keepeth the law, happy is he."* Without a clear vision and aggressive pursuit of your destiny, you risk falling into complacency and criticism rather than making a meaningful impact.

CHAPTER THREE

FATHERS ARE A GUIDING STAFF

"Fathers are the shoulders upon which we stand to see further, guiding us beyond our limitations into divine wisdom."

Seeing Further Through Their Shoulders

I saac Newton once said that if we have seen further, we stand on the shoulders of those who came before us. This isn't just some fancy talk; it's the real deal regarding spiritual growth. By standing on the shoulders of those who are seers, you gain the ability to see even further, but don't think it's all about the good stuff - you can also learn from the experiences of those who have made mistakes. For example, Solomon's wisdom was directly influenced by his father, David. Solomon didn't come out of nowhere; he learned from David's triumphs and failures. Proverbs 4:1-7 (KJV) says, "Hear, ye children, the instruction of a father, and attend to know understanding. For I give you good doctrine, forsake ye not my law, for I was my father's son, tender and only beloved in the sight of my mother. He also taught me and said, " Let thine heart retain my words: keep my commandments, and live." Can you see the words "He taught me and said unto me"? This is why we have Fathers; it is so that we can be taught.

Looking around, why do you think some people stay stuck in poverty? They have let it become their permanent business partner, like a bad habit they can't shake off.

I learned something crucial from my spiritual father, and you knew it, too. "Developing professional work habits is key to keeping poverty from setting up shop in your life." When I say professional work habits, I'm not just talking about showing up on time and wearing a tie. I'm talking about a whole mindset, a way of living that combines spiritual wisdom with being smart and intelligent. As you understand God's ways and sharpen your discernment, you should learn how to apply that wisdom to your everyday life. And like I have been saying from the beginning, you don't have to make all life's mistakes yourself. If something worked for someone else, it could probably work for you, and if a father failed before you, then there's every possibility you may also fail by applying that strategy.

Let's break it down: in Proverbs 24:30-32, which we read before, what gave poverty permanent residency in this man's life? It wasn't bad luck or the economy or any of that nonsense. It was the ignoring of work ethics, plain and simple. When you disregard work ethics, you might as well roll out the red carpet for poverty because you are inviting it to be your new business partner. You can try to explain it away and make excuses all you want, but at the end of the day, you will end up a loser. The way that this laziness creeps into many people is that they fall into the clutches of procrastination. I can assure you that if you keep putting off the work you should do today, thinking you will get it done tomorrow, then that tomorrow will never come. It's like chasing the horizon, but if you take these lessons to heart and let them sink in, your life will automatically get on the right track.

Let's look at verse 35 of Proverbs 25; you might be scratching your head, wondering what this has to do with anything, but trust me, it's essential. The Bible says, *"It is the glory of God to conceal a thing: but the honor of kings is to search out a matter."* Now, let that sink in for a minute. No lazy man ever achieved anything worthwhile, did they? Your life, my friend, is determined by the revelation that is revealed to you. And here's the thing, God's decided not to keep revelation out in the open where any Tom, Dick, or Harry can stumble upon it. No, sir. He hides it and tucks it away so that only the serious, the hungry, and the passionate can discover it. You will find it only when you search for it with all your heart, like a man dying of thirst searches for water in the desert. More often than not, it will take a spiritual father for you to see it finally; sometimes, you will see it and not understand it; at this point, you will need the guiding staff, that is, your spiritual father, to help you truly understand and see where God is taking you to.

Why don't losers value treasure? I'll tell you why. It's because every time they seek treasure, it's always at their beck and call. When something seems to cost them almost nothing, they don't pay it any attention or value it, and before you know it, it gets neglected like yesterday's newspaper. But that's a fool's game, and you need to know God's word, vision, and revelations, for your life can never be treated or searched for in such a way. Proverbs 2:4-5 says, *"If thou seekest her as silver, and searchest for her as for hid treasures; Then shalt thou understand the fear of the Lord, and find the knowledge of God."* You will have to approach it like a prospector panning for gold, sifting through every word and every verse, looking for that nugget of truth that will change your life, and often, you will need guidance as you do it.

You must ask yourself, what is the lesson my spiritual father is trying to teach me today? What treasures have they hidden in their words? Sometimes, we fail to recognize the value of the wisdom we receive because we don't see its immediate benefit. However, just as the Bible says in Proverbs 23:23 (KJV), *"Buy the truth, and sell it not; also wisdom, and instruction, and understanding."* Truth and wisdom must be cherished, even when their immediate benefits aren't apparent. Today, a generation has lost the art of learning from fathers. We see young people wanting to figure things out independently and believing the old ways are outdated. But Scripture reminds us in Ecclesiastes 1:9-10 (KJV), *"The thing that hath been, it is that which shall be; and that which is done is that which shall be done: and there is no new thing under the sun."* The challenges we face today are not new. The spiritual battles, trials, and temptations are the same, just wearing different masks. This is why it is imperative to stand on the shoulders of our spiritual fathers and mothers; they have already faced these battles and can guide us through them.

Fathers help us not only see further but also endure longer. There is something about the strength of a father figure, whether a biological father, a mentor, or a spiritual guide, that gives us the endurance to push forward when we feel like giving up. They act as a "guiding staff," something we can lean on when our strength fails. Isaiah 40:29-31 (KJV) says, *"He giveth power to the faint, and them that have no might he increaseth strength... they that wait upon the LORD shall renew their strength; they shall mount up with wings as eagles; they shall run, and not be weary; and they shall walk, and not faint."* Fathers help us wait on the Lord and receive that renewed strength.

Ultimately, we must learn from spiritual fathers that we cannot do this alone. God did not design us to walk the spiritual journey in isolation. We are part of a larger body, a family of believers with spiritual fathers to guide us. The Bible constantly refers to God's people as a family, a community. Romans 12:5 (KJV) states, *"So we, being many, are one body in Christ, and every member one of another."* In this family, fathers hold a special place. They help us see further, guide us through storms, and keep us grounded in the Word of God.

Service Leads To Blessings

Service in the house of God is not just a task we undertake to fulfill obligations; it is the key to unlocking divine blessings and favor. We see this principle laid out time and again in Scripture, where those who serve faithfully are rewarded in this life and eternity. When God instructed Moses to build the Tabernacle, He called for skilled individuals like Bezalel to oversee the work, but what is often overlooked is that Bezalel's service was not just about physical labor but a spiritual assignment, an act of worship. Exodus 31:2-3 (KJV) says, *"See, I have called by name Bezalel the son of Uri, the son of Hur, of the tribe of Judah: And I have filled him with the spirit of God, in wisdom, and understanding, and knowledge, and in all manner of workmanship."* The Lord had filled Bezalel with His Spirit to complete the work of the Tabernacle, and this tells us something important: that God always empowers those willing to serve. He does not leave us to do the work of the ministry in our strength. This is true not just for building physical structures but also for building His Kingdom. Whatever role you have in the church, whether cleaning the sanctuary, greeting people at the door, or leading a prayer group, I want you to know that it is not insignificant; you are filled with the Spirit of God to fulfill your assignment. And with that comes divine favor.

This divine appointment carries a powerful lesson for us today: when you come to the house of God, do not come merely as a passive member. No, you must come as one filled with the Spirit of God, ready to serve with all your heart, mind, and strength. Romans 12:11 says, *"Not slothful in business; fervent in spirit; serving the Lord."* This appeals to us to approach our service to God with the same diligence and enthusiasm we would apply to our most critical earthly endeavors and even our corporate businesses.

I implore you, especially if you are a handyman with professional skills, as much as you can. Always inspect the house of God at least every month and step out of your comfort zone because it stretches beyond our growth limits. This beloved is what God is looking for; he desires believers willing to go above and beyond in their service. You may think, "But I cannot stand up and preach as you do." Hear me well; you have a role, a unique and vital assignment in the body of Christ. Your task may be to protect the house of God or serve in ways that are "background" in nature; don't relent. And let me be clear: if you do not fulfill your role, God will find another to take your place. This is not a threat but a statement of truth born out of years of observing the workings of God's kingdom. But if you do, you can be sure that God's blessings await you.

Your work may not always be seen or appreciated by those around you today. But these acts of service, these seemingly small gestures of faithfulness, are the foundations upon which God builds our favor. Consider Bezalel's lineage for a moment. His grandfather, Hur, was one of the men who held up Moses' arms during the battle against the Amalekites (Exodus 17:12-13 KJV). Hur's simple act of holding up Moses' arms led to Israel's victory. This seemingly small action carried generational blessings, and Bezalel's opportunity to lead the construction of the Tabernacle and become highly blessed by the Lord directly resulted from his grandfather's faithfulness. The lesson here is clear: service brings personal blessings and leaves a legacy for generations to come.

Many of you have tried hard, and for this, we give thanks, but I must ask: at what point should you stop trying and serving God? If you were to ask me when I should stop praying, stop preaching to the people God has placed under me, or stop breathing, I would say, "Never!" As long as there is breath in my lungs and as long as I draw breath on this earth, I will be on the Lord's side and continue to serve Him. Even if you live to be 120 or 130 years old, that span is brief compared to the vastness of eternity. Moses and his generation lived long lives by our standards, but it has been over 4,000 years since they walked this earth, and yet, here we are, still speaking of them and drawing lessons from their lives of service and obedience. Many times, we look for recognition in the wrong places. We want people to see what we do and acknowledge our efforts. But the Bible teaches us that it is not man's applause that matters but God's approval. In Matthew 6:4 (KJV), Jesus says,

"That thine alms may be in secret: and thy Father which seeth in secret himself shall reward thee openly." God sees what we do in secret, and He rewards us openly. We must serve faithfully, even when no one is watching. Our reward comes from God, not man.

A Father Teaches You How To Serve God And Guides You Along The Way

A father's role is not just to provide for physical needs or offer emotional support; a father's primary duty is to guide his children in the ways of the Lord; this means fathers teach us how to serve God and, through their example, we learn how to walk in faith, obey God's instructions, and fulfill our divine assignments accurately. God positions them to show us the acceptable and perfect way to serve God. When you think about service to God, you must recognize that there are different service levels; some serve God out of obligation, others out of fear, and others out of love and devotion.

Some of the ways include;

Not serving Him at all: This is the most dangerous of all. Not serving God at all means ignoring His, neglecting His instructions, and ultimately, setting yourself up for failure and eventual destruction. Matthew 25:30 speaks of the unprofitable servant cast into outer darkness because he did nothing with the talents his master gave him. This means that not serving God is a direct path to spiritual poverty.

The excellent way to serve God: This is where many believers find themselves; it is a position where they serve God, but their service is half-hearted. They do enough to fulfill obligations, but there is no passion, no zeal. These are the people in Revelation 3:15-16, the ones whom the scripture warns against lukewarm service because although they are serving, they are freezing, but at least they are better than the other group. *"I know thy works, that thou art neither cold nor hot: I would thou wert cold or hot. So then, because thou art* *lukewarm and neither cold nor hot, I will spue thee out of my mouth."* Good service is commendable, but it is not enough to bring about the fullness of God's blessings.

The acceptable way to serve God: This is where our service begins to fall in line with God's expectations. It is the place where we serve with reverence, humility, and a desire to please God. Hebrews 12:28 (KJV) says, *"Wherefore we receiving a kingdom which cannot be moved, let us have grace, whereby we may serve God acceptably with reverence and godly fear."* Acceptable service is marked by sincerity, devotion, and a heart that seeks to honor God in everything.

The perfect way to serve God: This is the highest level of service; it is not just acceptable; it is ideal because it is motivated by love and complete surrender to God's will. In this type of service, there is no holding back. Everything we are and have is given to God for His glory. Matthew 22:37-38 (KJV) defines this level of service by saying, *"Thou shalt love the Lord thy God with all thy heart, and with all thy soul, and with all thy mind. This is the first and great commandment."* When we serve God in this perfect way, we are open to experiencing His blessings not only in our lives but also in the lives of our descendants.

My highest desire is to serve God in the perfect way. This is not a boast but a declaration of intent, a commitment to pursue the highest form of devotion possible, and I tell you truthfully, when you set your heart on serving God in this manner, the blessings that flow not only to you but also to your lineage are immeasurable.

Take Timothy, for example; he was a young believer about whom the Apostle Paul spoke highly. In 2 Timothy 1:5, Paul said, *"When I call to remembrance the unfeigned faith that is in thee, which dwelt first in thy grandmother Lois, and thy mother Eunice; and I am persuaded that in thee also."* This is a beautiful illustration of faith passed down through generations, from grandmother to mother to son.

As a teenager, Timothy was entrusted with the pastorship of a church numbering some 30,000 members. By the time he reached his twenties, under his faithful stewardship, that congregation must have grown to an astounding 61,000 souls. His spiritual father, Paul, encouraged him with these words found in 1 Timothy 4:12, *"Let no man despise thy youth; but be thou an example of the believers, in word, in conversation, in charity, in spirit, in faith, in purity."* Why was Timothy successful? Because he had an example to follow, a pattern of solid faith passed down through his family line, beginning with his grandmother Lois, who imparted it to his mother, Eunice. This legacy of faith, nurtured and guided by his spiritual father, Paul, was what bore fruit in Timothy's life in remarkable ways. When you look at this, you will see that if you do not have a spiritual father, you will be greatly limited because there are several guidance that God can only bring to you through a "man" because God will not come down and give it to you.

As I reflect on these truths, I feel a stirring in my spirit, a divine compulsion to pray for every parent here today, whether you have adopted children or biological ones. From this moment forward, I declare in the mighty name of Jesus that any spirit attempting to lead your children astray or sow seeds of doubt in their minds is arrested and banished. For those among us who yearn to become parents, I proclaim supernatural fertility. In the name of Jesus, you will have your children; whatever obstacles may seem impossible, we cancel those impossibilities by the power of Christ.

Through the guiding hands of your spiritual father, God can call you higher, beckoning you to "Come up hither, and I will show you deep things that will happen later." I pray fervently that the spirit of the Lord will capture your children and that in your lifetime, your obedience to God will bear fruit in their lives, making perfect sense of all your sacrifices and devotion.

Heed this warning, beloved: anything that weakens God's instruction to you will inevitably hinder the construction of your destiny, and anything that can stop you from fully adhering to your father's instructions has successfully done this damage to you.

Although following His instructions may not always feel comfortable and may not even align with human logic or worldly wisdom, I want you to know that it is the surest path to true prosperity and fulfillment. You must understand that when God desires to bestow great treasure upon you, He often wraps that treasure in instructions that may seem nonsensical to the natural mind. Your task, guided by the wisdom of your spiritual fathers, is to follow those instructions with faith and obedience. If you choose to forge your path, disregarding the guidance of your spiritual fathers and the explicit instructions of God's Word, you will inevitably pay a high price. However, if you humbly submit to His ways, if you faithfully follow the path illuminated by your spiritual fathers, you will still face challenges - for this is the nature of spiritual growth, but the price will be so discounted and so mitigated by God's grace that you will stand in awe of His goodness.

CHAPTER FOUR

AVOIDING THE FOLLY
OF THE RAT RACE

"True greatness is not in the hustle, but in obedience and submission to God's will, guided by spiritual authority."

In Followership Lies Your Greatness

If you have been running from pillar to post looking for a breakthrough, you have missed something important. You have been wasting your time. We call this the rat race. Let me explain how it works. Imagine you put a piece of cheese on a string and tie it to a rat's tail; the rat will smell it and want to catch it right. But here's the thing: that cheese is always just out of reach because the more the rat tries to reach the cheese, the more it keeps going in circles and circles, trying to catch its tail. Meanwhile, All the rat needs to do is turn around and take one bite, but instead, it keeps chasing after the smell of the cheese. The rat gets dizzier and dizzier as time passes, trapped in its pursuit. The painful part is that a rat may survive this dizziness for a day, but give it two, three, or four days, and that rat is dead. Can you follow what I'm saying here? You may never get those things as long as you intend to spend your life pursuing things. God never intended for us to function that way.

This rat race was what he stepped into when he decided to ignore God's instructions and started following his ideas. He chased after that cheese into Egypt, and when he finally caught it, he found himself trapped in a snare. Isaac was about to make the same mistake, but God stepped in and said, "No, don't go down." So I'm telling you, whatever has programmed your downward movement, whatever it is that you may have been chasing, it's time for you to stop and start following.

What are you running after in life? So often, people chase after what appears to be success, wealth, or fame, believing that achieving these things will bring fulfillment. But the truth is, real greatness and true success lie not in chasing after the things of this world but in aligning ourselves with God's purpose and following His path, especially when a spiritual father is giving us the necessary guidance. Pursuing worldly things will leave you in constant exhaustion, disappointment, and spiritual emptiness, so instead of running aimlessly after the wrong things, you should anchor yourself in God's direction and follow as he leads every day.

The Blessings Are Meant To Follow You

Psalm 23:6 (KJV) says, "Surely goodness and mercy shall follow me all the days of my life." Notice the wording here: goodness and mercy shall follow us, not the other way around. When you are in alignment with God's will, blessings will pursue you; you don't need to chase them. It's not about the hustle or the struggle to gain what you think you need. It's actually about trust, obedience, and followership.

One clear example of followership is in Jesus' call to His disciples in Matthew 4:19 (KJV): *"And he saith unto them, follow me, and I will make you fishers of men."* Jesus didn't say, "Chase after fame, wealth, or power, and they will make you great." He simply said, "Follow me." The greatness of the disciples was not in their earthly pursuits but in their dedication to following Christ. Their transformation into "fishers of men" came from their obedience and submission to His leadership. Likewise, when you submit to Christ's leadership and those He has placed as spiritual authorities in your life, you can be sure you are well-positioned for greatness.

When you finally grasp the reality that true greatness comes from followership, you will also begin to see that your greatness is tied to the spiritual authority you follow because "men make men." I have said this before and will say again, "The outcome of your life will largely depend on who you follow." Just as the disciples were transformed by following Jesus, and Elisha inherited a double portion of Elijah's spirit by following his master closely, we are also shaped by the people we follow and the fathers we submit to.

That's why staying connected to the proper spiritual lineage is crucial and should not be bargained; I am blessed to be part of a spiritual lineage that transforms lives, just as the apostles followed the teachings of Jesus Christ and received the Holy Spirit, which empowered them to do great things. Look at Moses and Joshua, Elijah and Elisha, Paul and Timothy, David and Samuel, and so on; in each case, the greatness of the followers was a direct result of their commitment to their spiritual leader, not because they chased after worldly things.

Strength Is Found In Followership

Coupled with all I have said, great strength comes from following God's plan; when you stay in line with God's plan by being a faithful follower, there is a divine strength to overcome challenges that will come your way. One of the blessings I have received from my Father is the continual renewal of strength because strength is something we all need, and it must be renewed constantly. When you receive this strength I am talking about, you can walk through a troop and leap over a wall. When you face walls, you are meant to break down; they will give up and leave before you even get there. Then, most of the energy you would've used to destroy those walls will instead be used to follow after God's divine vision and pursue your God-given purpose. This happens when a person follows the path of submission to fathers; you can accomplish more if you connect to the instructions from the fathers and their impartations.

So don't chase after the wrong things, and don't get caught up in the rat race; instead, follow God's path, learn from those He's placed in your life, and watch how He uses that to bring you into your greatness. Because in followership lies your greatness. It's not about always trying to be out front, always trying to be the leader. Sometimes, the most significant thing you can do is humble yourself, follow, and learn. That's where true greatness lies.

The Feet Of The Fathers Are Where True Wisdom Lies

Seek Wisdom at All Costs

Now, let's look at verses 11 and 12 of Job 28. *"He bindeth the floods from overflowing; and the thing that is hid bringeth he forth to light. But where shall wisdom be found? and where is the place of understanding?"* Did you see that question? But where can anyone find wisdom? Where can we get understanding? You must know that your treasure is tied to your understanding. If you don't know, you won't have experience, and you cannot mine the treasures of life. Most people without understanding are often living in confusion, And guess what? They follow their paths. That's why the path of God may not feel comfortable; it may not seem easy. But I'm telling you the truth: if you follow the path of God, even when it doesn't feel comfortable, it secures your future.

In another scripture, Proverbs 4:7 says, "Wisdom is the principal thing; therefore, get wisdom: and with all thy getting get understanding." This shows us how vital wisdom and understanding are. Then, in James 1:5, we read, *"If any of you lack wisdom, let him ask of God, that giveth to all men liberally, and upbraideth not; and it shall be given him."* God is ready to give us wisdom if we ask for it. And Proverbs 3:13-14 says, *"Happy is the man that findeth wisdom, and the man that getteth understanding. For the merchandise of it is better than the merchandise of silver, and the gain thereof than fine gold."* This tells us that wisdom and understanding are more valuable than silver and gold.

When running around chasing after things, remember that what you are looking for might be closer than you think. It might be in the wisdom and understanding that comes from following God's path and listening to the father he has placed over your life. Don't get caught up in the rat race; always chasing after the next big thing. Instead, see what God has already placed in your hands, mind, and spirit. That's where your real treasure lies.

Look at Job 28:13-15 (NIV): *"No mortal comprehends its worth; it cannot be found in the land of the living. The deep says, 'It is not in me'; the sea says, 'It is not with me. It cannot be bought with the finest gold, nor can its price be weighed out in silver."* The pursuit of wisdom has been a timeless quest for humanity, yet so often, we look for it in all the wrong places, and this scripture is unequivocal that wisdom cannot be found through the typical means people seek in this world. Wisdom, and I mean true wisdom, is not something you can dig out of the earth or extract from the seas. It is not gained through academic pursuit or worldly knowledge. It cannot be bought with gold or silver. Yet, despite this indescribable nature, wisdom is available to those seeking it right at spiritual fathers' feet.

In Proverbs 4:1-2 (KJV), You must understand that the instructions and wisdom passed down from spiritual fathers are not to be taken lightly; they are the keys to navigating life's complexities and finding success in every physical and spiritual endeavor.

Proverbs 3:13-14 (KJV) says it *"is more precious than rubies, and all the things thou canst desire are not to be compared unto her."* This is why it is essential to recognize that the impartation of wisdom from our spiritual fathers is far more valuable than any material wealth we could ever acquire. No amount of gold, silver, or precious stones can match the worth of wisdom from those who have walked with God for years, learning directly from His hand. Through Connecting to spiritual impartation, you are tapping into a treasure far beyond what the world can offer. Still, the key to receiving this impartation lies in the purity of our hearts. We don't give money or honor to our spiritual fathers to buy wisdom; that's impossible. Instead, we honor them as a way of connecting to the grace and wisdom they carry, understanding that what we receive from them is a gift that cannot be earned or bought. This is why 1 Peter 5:5 (KJV) instructs us, saying, *"Submit yourselves unto the elder. Yea, all of you be subject one to another and be clothed with humility."* In humility and submission, you can position yourself to receive the impartations and spiritual deposits from a father, including the wisdom needed for life and purpose.

When you spend time in the presence of a spiritual father, whether in a personal meeting, during a church service, or even through their teachings, you are tapping into decades of experience, insight, and divine revelation. Something the 50 years cannot give you can easily be gotten just by spending 5 hours and even fewer times with them, and what could have taken you years to understand on your own is given to you in moments. Proverbs 13:20 (KJV)

Spiritual Insulation

You should also realize that lessons from your spiritual father are meant to insulate you from the foolishness that often accompanies youth or inexperience. Each of us has, at some point, walked the path of foolishness. It's a part of life but not where we are meant to stay. When you submit to the wisdom of those who have gone before you, you will begin to graduate from what I call the "university of stupidity." This is how you will move from making mistakes born out of ignorance to living a life marked by dignity and discernment.

You should also realize that your foolishness is not always about blatant sin or rebellion. Sometimes, foolishness can manifest as a simple lack of understanding or poor decision-making, but wisdom in our lives changes everything. It elevates us, allowing us to make choices that lead to honor and respect. Proverbs 24:3-4 (KJV) says, *"Through wisdom is a house built; and by understanding it is established: And by knowledge shall the chambers be filled with all precious and pleasant riches."* Wisdom builds our lives, homes, relationships, and ministries. Without it, we are left to stumble through life, making costly mistakes.

Child of God, imparting wisdom is a sacred process that cannot be rushed. Often, the most amazing moments of wisdom come not in formal teaching settings but in simple, everyday moments spent at the feet of our fathers. Just like Elisha was committed to following Elijah closely, refusing to leave his side even when others tried to dissuade him in 2 Kings 2:9-10, in the same way, you must be willing to commit yourself to the process of learning from your spiritual father. This means being patient, humble, and willing to wait for the right time to receive the wisdom and impartation they carry. It cannot be forced or rushed, but it transforms your life in ways you could never have achieved when you received it.

When you receive this kind of wisdom from your spiritual father, you receive a treasure that will last a lifetime; it cannot be stolen or depreciated over time. The more you use it, the more valuable it becomes, and as you apply this wisdom in your life, you will see changes, you will start making better decisions, you will start seeing things from a different perspective, and you will begin to understand things that used to confuse you. Another beautiful part is that as you grow in this wisdom, you will become a source of knowledge for others and be able to impart what has been imparted to you. This is how the kingdom of God grows and how we build a legacy that lasts beyond our lifetime.

So, don't underestimate the value of sitting at the feet of your spiritual father, don't ever think it's a waste of time, and don't think you have better things to do. There's nothing more valuable you could be doing than receiving wisdom that will shape your life and the lives of generations to come.

When you sit at the feet of your spiritual father, you are not just hearing words; you are receiving an impartation, a mantle, an anointing, and something that will change your life forever.

CHAPTER FIVE

DEALING WITH
FATHERS

"To follow a spiritual father is to learn without resistance; in obedience lies the path to honor."

Learn Rather Than Argue

W hen a Father feels you are acting stupid or stupid, he may begin to avoid you, especially if he has corrected you several times and you are refusing to make corrections. This is because wise men and great men value their peace. Being great exposes you to many challenges, so you must seek relationships with productive people. It is said that wisdom leads one to silence, whereas folly leads to argument. When Jesus said, "Every branch in me that beareth not fruit he taketh away" (John 15:2, KJV), He meant it because He didn't want to waste opportunities that others could use. So here's the question: are you willing to be baptized in the discipline needed to heed fathers and become wise?

In Matthew 20:23, Jesus said, *"Ye shall drink indeed of my cup, and be baptized with the baptism that I am baptized with: but to sit on my right hand, and on my left, is not mine to give, but it shall be given* to them for whom it is prepared of my Father" (KJV). This shows that you can attend church and serve at the end of the day, but as a father, I decide your placement. You can serve and still have a disloyal heart. In life, there must come a time when wisdom dictates that we must learn rather than argue and submit rather than resist. Jesus asked His disciples in Matthew 20:22 (KJV), "Are ye able to drink of the cup that I shall drink of?" He was challenging them to see beyond the surface of their ambitions and understand the weight of the suffering and responsibility that comes with honor and position rather than argue about who will have the position. Too often, we argue when we ought to be learning, and we keep resisting correction because our pride closes our eyes to the wisdom behind it. But Jesus, knowing the hearts of His disciples, reminded them that they indeed would share in His suffering, not because they argued their way into it, but because they were being prepared for something greater than they could understand at that moment.

You see, preparation in life is critical, and it is during this time that we are most tested; what many consider as temptation is just a test of their character under pressure because just as gold is refined through fire, we are shaped by the challenges we face, but only if we approach them with a heart willing to learn. If you resist, you will remain unformed, unprepared, and unfit for the honor that awaits you. The Bible says to us in Proverbs 3:11-12 (KJV), "My son, despise not the chastening of the LORD; neither be weary of his correction: For whom the LORD loveth he correcteth; even as a father the son in whom he delighteth." If you are a wise child, you will learn to accept correction without argument, understanding that your father's rebuke is not a rejection but a tool for your growth.

A heart unwilling to learn will eventually become a reason for destruction, whether in the family, relationships, or life. Jesus pointed out this truth in the parable of the unfaithful servant in Luke 12:42-46 (KJV). The servant, left in charge while his master was away, began to mistreat those under him, assuming his master would delay his return. However, when the master returned unexpectedly, the servant faced harsh punishment, not only for his actions but for failing to learn from the master's teachings. This servant's mistake was not just in his behavior but in his refusal to understand his role as a steward. In his heart, he argued against the responsibilities entrusted to him, believing he could act as he pleased. His lack of humility and teachability cost him everything.

This is a lesson for all of us, and you must take it seriously! When you resist correction and argue rather than learn from your father, you miss out on the opportunities to grow into the roles and blessings God has prepared for you. Proverbs 13:18 (KJV) says, *"Poverty and shame shall be to him that refuseth instruction: but he that regardeth reproof shall be honored."* Whether spiritual or biological, a father's correction is meant to guide you, not hurt or destroy you. It is easy to fall into the trap of believing that discipline is rejection, but truthfully, it is the clearest sign of love and investment. Fathers, like God, desire their children to prosper, but that prosperity can only come through learning, not arguing.

Spiritual Lineage And Mentorship

The wisdom and impartation passed down through spiritual generations to a son is invaluable. Still, it can only be received by those willing to listen, absorb, and apply it. When I traveled to Nigeria to visit my spiritual father, some questioned the wisdom of such a journey. They could not understand why I would go to such lengths for something that, in their eyes, seemed unnecessary. But wisdom is often foolishness to those who are not seeking it. 1 Corinthians 1:25 (KJV) says, *"Because the foolishness of God is wiser than men, and the weakness of God is stronger than men."* Worldly standards cannot measure the wisdom and impartation I received from that trip. It was an impartation to benefit me and those who come after me. I can assure you that my generation will never recover from it.

All these are reasons why, as far as I am concerned, a child who argues with his father, especially his spiritual father, is cutting themselves off from this flow of wisdom and impartation. The Bible is filled with examples of those who prospered because they submitted to the wisdom of their fathers. Isaac obeyed Abraham and, in doing so, inherited the blessings promised to his father (Genesis 26:3). When you look at my submission to my father. You think I'm not doing something right; that burden rests on your heart, but I assure you that I strive to be 100% right by God's grace. If it were my time to leave this earth tomorrow, I would stand confidently in heaven. I was reflecting on something profound regarding trust and wisdom. I remembered an African parable that says, "When a little child knows how to run errands for the elders, that child will be allowed to sit down and eat dinner with them without even washing his hands." This shows how elders value children who can be entrusted with important tasks and that the child is wise and responsible. As much as you can, avoid anything that might cause strife or make your father feel like you are a burden to him. You don't want to be the child who brings pain to their father's soul.

Learning from a father is a lifetime process; it is not something we do once and move on from; it is a continuous journey of growth, correction, and improvement. As long as you are willing to listen and to receive instruction without resistance, you will continue to grow and prosper. Jesus Himself, though He was the Son of God, did not argue with His Father but submitted fully to His will. In John 5:19 (KJV), Jesus said, *"Verily, verily, I say unto you, The Son can do nothing of himself, but what he seeth the Father do: for what things soever he doeth, these also doeth the Son likewise."* Even the Son of God understood the importance of learning from the Father, so how can you begin to think you can survive without taking your spiritual Father seriously?

Proverbs 15:31, *"The ear that heareth the reproof of life abideth among the wise" (KJV).* By being open to reproof and guidance, you position yourself among those who are wise and can benefit from the experiences and insights of our elders. Also, learning rather than arguing creates an environment conducive to spiritual growth and maturity. This approach helps you build a deeper relationship with your father and allows you to tap into the wealth of wisdom they possess; this is not just about avoiding conflict; it's about being able to touch their spirit so that you can partake of the rich deposits that their father and father's father have deposited on their lives. Don't forget there's a long lineage of spiritual ancestry before you, where several anointings have consistently been passed down from one generation to another.

It's important to know that this principle of learning rather than arguing doesn't mean you are never to ask questions or seek clarification. Asking thoughtful questions is a vital part of the learning process. The difference lies in our attitude and intention. Are you asking questions to gain understanding, or are you questioning to challenge authority and assert your opinions? The former leads to growth, while the latter often leads to conflict and stagnation.

The choice is yours. You can argue, resist, and ultimately miss out on the blessings and wisdom from your fathers, or you can humble yourself, learn, and be elevated to new levels of understanding and glory. Learning rather than arguing is not always easy, but it is the path of wisdom, honor, and lasting success.

Fathers Empower You For Speedy Results

The empowerment that comes from a father is one of the most powerful tools for achieving swift results in life and destiny because your spiritual fathers possess a unique empowerment from God to propel you forward beyond comprehension and natural understanding. This is the essence of a father's empowerment. It's not just about giving direction; it's about providing guidance that leads to results that would otherwise take years to achieve.

The empowerment of a father not only saves time but also positions you in a place where you can flourish regardless of external circumstances. Like Isaac, many of us face situations where things around us seem to be failing. Perhaps there's a financial drought, a relational breakdown, or even a spiritual famine. I want you to know that in moments such as these, a single declaration from a father can alter the course of your life, bringing about supernatural acceleration and results that are powered by the hand of God. This is why it's important to remain close to those who have been set as fathers in your life. They carry the keys to your destiny, and through their prayer, laying of hands, prophecy, and declaration, you can steer through life's challenges with ease and speed.

When circumstances are often pressing on us, we make decisions out of fear and anxiety because we usually think we must act quickly to avoid disaster. In doing so, we leave the position where God has planted us. Consider Isaac wanting to leave the land. God wanted him to stay all because of the famine, but God, acting as his Father, stepped in and said, "That's the wrong move." And how often do we make moves that take us out of God's intended path in moments of fear or confusion? This is why listening to a father's counsel is essential; he often sees what we cannot. Proverbs 12:15 (KJV) *"The way of a fool is right in his own eyes: but he that hearkeneth unto counsel is wise."*

As human beings, we are not just passive recipients of life's events; instead, God created us with the ability to make choices. We have the authority to make choices, but through a father's blessing, we gain the wisdom to make the right ones. Take, for example, the *In Vitro Fertilization* (IVF) process. In the natural world, the gender of a child is determined by chance, but through IVF, parents are given the option to choose the gender of their baby. This scientific advancement mirrors the spiritual truth that, with the empowerment of a father, we can make selections in life that align with God's purpose for us. We are not left to chance. The Father's blessing gives us the right to say, "I want this; I reject that."

This spiritual empowerment far exceeds what science can offer; while science strives to catch up with the wisdom of God, spiritual truths often surpass the limitations of human knowledge. Think about the technology we have today, like Wi-Fi, which came late to many parts of the world. In Africa, long before these modern communication methods were invented, people used mirrors to communicate spiritually. What seemed advanced to some was already being practiced in a different form elsewhere. Similarly, when you operate under a father's blessing and guidance, you are spiritually ahead of the curve, accessing truths and revelations that may seem out of reach to the natural mind.

Now, here's the revelation I don't want you to miss: through the IVF process, couples can select the gender of their babies. However, there was a woman long ago who achieved gender selection without doctors but with the covering of her father. I am talking about Hannah, the mother of Samuel, the bible tells us that she prayed and cried before the Lord, and when Eli, her spiritual covering, came in, he simply said to her, "GO." It's done, and that was all. She not only got a child, she got a male child as desired. Something that would have been impossible if her father had not spoken.

I tell you the truth: Fatherly blessings, prophetic blessings, and priestly coverings always give you the upper hand in selecting what you want and deleting what you don't want from your life and destiny.

Look at the story of Jacob and his father, Isaac. For example, Jacob's life changed drastically after receiving his father's blessing. In Genesis 27, Isaac's blessing on Jacob was so powerful that it altered his life. Esau sought the same blessing, but it could not be reversed once it was given to Jacob. This shows the irrevocable nature of a father's empowerment; it sets you on a path that no one can take away, and the speed at which Jacob's life unfolded after that blessing was remarkable. Though he faced challenges, the blessing propelled him forward in ways that his efforts never could have.

But it's not just about receiving blessings; it's also about maintaining a heart that is ready to receive. This is where loyalty and humility come into play. Many people serve faithfully but with divided hearts. They may call someone "father" or "mentor," but their actions and attitudes reveal a lack of submission. I once told one of my sons, "You call me Daddy, but I've never asked you to change your schedule for something important." The empowerment of a father is only as effective as the heart that receives it. A divided heart cannot fully embrace the blessing, so the speed of empowerment is slowed. A loyal heart, however, will see rapid progress, much like Isaac did when he obeyed the voice of God and stayed in Gerar.

That's not all; a father's blessing provides protection and guidance. In Numbers 6:24-26, we see the priestly blessing that God instructed Aaron and his sons to pronounce over the Israelites: *"The Lord bless thee, and keep thee: The Lord make his face shine upon thee, and be gracious unto thee: The Lord lift his countenance upon thee, and give thee peace"* (KJV). This blessing encapsulates protection, favor, and peace, all essential for achieving speedy results in life. Now, I need to repeat this quickly: as I talk about fathers. However, material blessings are inclusive; I do not want you to make the mistake of limiting what I am saying to just material prosperity. Don't forget that you have a divine destiny to fulfill, and that's God's ultimate purpose and desire.

I am simply saying that the empowerment that comes from a father's blessing is not just about material prosperity or quick success; it's about positioning you in line with God's purpose and timing for your life because when your spiritual father blesses and speaks into your life, he essentially agrees with God's plan for your life. This agreement creates a spiritual atmosphere that accelerates the manifestation of God's promises over you. Don't forget that a father's blessing carries the weight of authority in the spirit, a mighty wand the Lord has granted them. In other words, when a father speaks a blessing over you, he is exercising his God-given authority to shape your destiny, and this authority, when properly used, can break generational curses, open doors of opportunity, and establish a legacy of righteousness. It is practically a manifestation of Proverbs 18:21, which tells us, *"Death and life are in the power of the tongue: and they that love it shall eat the fruit thereof"* (KJV). A father's words of blessing carry life-giving power that can propel you toward destiny at an accelerated pace.

Your father's blessing is a powerful tool for empowering speedy results in your life. As you recognize and embrace the power of your fatherly blessings, you can experience accelerated growth and success in your spiritual and natural endeavors. As children an actual child, you must remain open to receiving this empowerment, knowing that through it, you are positioned to achieve results far beyond what you could accomplish on your own.

CHAPTER SIX

THE MYSTERY OF FAMILY AND BLESSINGS

"Generational blessings flow through you when you honor the lineage of wisdom passed down from those who came before."

The Blessings Of A Father Ultimately Flows To The Children

When God spoke to Abraham, He said, "I will bless you." Do you realize that This blessing was not just for Abraham but also for his family? God has family in mind when He blesses, and because of this, anyone who is family-conscious captures God's attention. Whether you belong to a nuclear family, an extended family, or even if you are a single parent, there is power in family unity. Isolation is one of the worst things you can do to yourself. The family has power, the power to uplift or to break. If opposing forces or a curse influences a family, that negativity can transfer to the next generation and continue to pass down. However, God is faithful, so He often raises one person in the family to break that cycle. Some of you may be facing tough battles, and you might be wondering why. The reason is that you are the pillar God has raised in your family.

Listen carefully; you must pay attention when a family member is constantly attacked. I'm not referring to those lazy and unwilling to put in the effort; I'm talking about the family members striving to make sense of their lives, yet they find themselves making three steps forward only to slip back seven steps. Instead of giving up, they keep pressing on. That ability to press forward despite the odds is itself a blessing. Often, this family member is "the star," "the light," and "the strength" of the family, and so they become the target of all sorts of attacks from the devil. God, in His kindness, chooses individuals to be the strength of their families. Do you understand? Sometimes it's just one person.

You may have been facing many battles, obstacles, and challenges. Well, I want you to know that you are probably the star and pillar of the family. The devil knows that the Lord has marked you to be the deliverer, and so he is doing all he can to bring you down or discourage you.

Look at Genesis 12:2-3 again, where God promises Abraham, "And I will make of thee a great nation, and I will bless thee, and make thy name great, and thou shalt be a blessing: And I will bless them that bless thee, and curse him that curseth thee: and in thee shall all families of the earth be blessed" (KJV). Do you see what I was talking about when I said The promise to Abraham was not just for him as an individual, but it was a blessing that would flow through him to his descendants and ultimately to all families of the earth? As a parent, you must never forget this as you serve God. As a child, you must continually strive to recognize the generational blessing on your family because just as there are generational curses, there are also generational blessings to be received.

The generational nature of blessings is a powerful reality we cannot overlook. When a father walks with God, his children benefit from that relationship. This is why we must never take the blessings and covering we receive from our fathers for granted. Whether it is a biological father, a spiritual father, or a mentor, the principle remains the same. Fathers carry a unique grace to pass down blessings that can shape their children's future. Think about Isaac and Jacob. Isaac received the blessing from Abraham, and he, in turn, passed that blessing down to his son, Jacob. That same blessing altered the course of Jacob's history, transforming him into Israel, the father of the twelve tribes.

Pursuing The Blessings

Take another look at Genesis 26, and you will realize that Isaac was living under the direct blessings of his father, Abraham. Verse 3 (KJV) reads, *"Sojourn in this land, and I will be with thee and will bless thee; for unto thee, and thy seed, I will give all these countries, and I will perform the oath which I sware unto Abraham, thy father."* Notice how God ties Isaac's blessing to His promise to Abraham. Isaac was living in the blessing not because of anything he had done but because of God's covenant with his father. This is how generational blessings work. A father's walk with God lays the foundation for his children to receive and walk in divine favor. So, do you have a father who can bless you? Don't forget this works both ways: a spiritual father and a physical father.

But don't forget that just because blessings are available in the spiritual or physical lineage doesn't mean they will automatically fall on you. NO! The blessing is available to the children but is not automatically received. The children must be positioned spiritually and mentally to receive what flows from their father. In Genesis 25, the story of Esau and Jacob cautions us that not everyone can receive blessings. Though Esau was the firstborn by rights and should have received God's first blessings and covenant with the family, he despised it. In Genesis 25:34 (KJV), after selling his birthright to Jacob, the Bible says, *"Esau despised his birthright."*

Esau didn't value the blessing of his father, and because of that, he lost it. Jacob, on the other hand, was determined to receive the blessing. Though his methods may have been questionable, his heart was in the right place because he valued what God had placed upon his father and pursued it with all his might. This is the same way Elisha pursued what was upon Elijah and the same way you should pursue what is on your Spiritual and physical father.

Esau's life should serve as a lesson to you that the blessings of a father are not to be taken lightly, seeing that God has designed fathers to be conduits of divine favor and provision, but it is up to the children to recognize and respect that. Just like Jacob, you must be hungry for the blessings that flow from your father. You must value the spiritual inheritance you receive and position yourself to receive it fully. When Proverbs 13:22 (KJV) says, *"A good man leaveth an inheritance to his children's children."* You must know and never forget that this inheritance is more than just material wealth; it's a spiritual heritage that can transform your life tremendously. In the natural world, the passing down of wealth from father to child is something that we are all familiar with; many families build legacies by ensuring that their children inherit both financial assets and the family business. But what is even more valuable than wealth is the wisdom, favor, and spiritual resources that can be received through impartation from a father (both spiritual and biological fathers). A father's blessing is a form of inheritance that cannot be quantified in material terms. It is a spiritual currency that grows and bears fruit long after the father has passed.

A Lesson From The Life Of Joseph

Look at the case of Joseph, the son of Jacob; Jacob had received the blessings of his father, Isaac, and that blessing flowed down to Joseph; even though Joseph was sold into slavery by his brothers, the blessing upon his life could not be hindered. In Genesis 39:2

(KJV), the Bible tells us, *"And the Lord was with Joseph, and he was a prosperous man."* This wasn't because of Joseph's position as an enslaved person; it was because of the blessing that was upon him; the blessing that Joseph carried was more potent than the circumstances he found himself in. That is the power of a father's blessing; it transcends situations and human limitations and guarantees divine results, even when everything seems to be against you.

In the New Testament, the bible also affirms this principle in Ephesians 6:2-3, by the commandment to honor our parents, *"which is the first commandment with promise; That it may be well with thee, and thou mayest live long on the earth"* (KJV). This shows that the relationship between parents (biological and spiritual) and children directly impacts blessings flow. With this in mind, let's consider the practical implications of this truth; when you truly understand this, it should motivate you to do several things:

- Seek reconciliation and healing in father-child relationships in case of brokenness or estrangement. Working towards restoration is essential, as it will unlock the flow of blessings.

- For fathers, there is a need to recognize the importance of living a life worthy of blessings. Your choices and actions have significant consequences for your children and future generations.

- Children must recognize the importance of honoring and respecting fathers, even when they are challenging. This posture of honor will position children to receive the blessings that flow from fatherhood.

- It should encourage everyone to see beyond our current and individual blessings to consider the generational impact of our obedience and fulfillment of God's purposes.

- For those who may not have had positive experiences with their biological fathers, it's time to recognize the importance of connecting with a spiritual father who can speak blessing and impart spiritual inheritance.

Recognize The Star In Your Children

Remember, I talked about God raising an individual in the family; in my case, God made it clear from the very beginning. I spent 12 months and two weeks in my mother's womb, and when I was finally born, my mother already knew everything about me. Among the nicest people in my family, she recognized me as her "star child." Yet, I became like a rebel and a gangster, opposite to my destiny. You see, for some of us, the devil knew our star from the beginning, and he attacked us terribly because his goal was to make sure that we did not fulfill our destiny. I pray that in your family, God will raise pure breeds, children who will not have to face some of the battles and attacks we did in our generation.

This is a crucial focus of the family altar. Establishing a family altar is one of the most important things you can do in your life and your family because if the destinies of your children, including the deliverance that God wants to bring, are to be preserved, then that altar must be needed. Don't worry; we will talk about this later.

Back to the main issue: as a parent, you must do all necessary to recognize your star kid. God places a sign on the star child whether you like it or not. Please note that this doesn't mean the other children will be useless or failures in life; that's far from what I am saying. If you are a saved parent, all your kids are meant to be stars; however, the Bible says, "Stars differ in glory" (1 Corinthians 15:41, KJV). And when I say you start kid, also know that I am not just talking about money or material success; I am talking about a particular child in that family on which the hand of God will be firm, and through that Child, God will always have a window in the family through which he can invade, bless, deliver, help and so much more.

Identifying this child is not something you can do with your brain. Still, by establishing a family altar, you will begin to interrupt contradictions, intercept complications, and interject against demonic activities that will want to ruin your family and God's generational blessings and purposes for that family. Your discernment of your children's lives will become heightened, and you will also be able to create protective coverings for them.

One way to identify the start child is their inclination towards spiritual things. Unfortunately, Satan is often aware of these star children and even attacks the parents first in most cases. He knows that if he can divide a marriage, he can plant seeds of discord in the hearts of the children, which will then lead to ruin in their lives. Sometimes, if he doesn't attack the marriage directly, he creates foolishness in one of the parents' minds. Have you seen parents who seem not to care about their children? Some even go to the extent of hurting that child; well, you should know Satan is at work. Think of someone like Joyce Meyer, for example; she was destined to change the world, so the devil attacked her even from the beginning in so many ways, seeking to destroy her.

Some mothers, fearing for their children, will say, "I won't let my child be around their father; fathers are terrible." Although you must use wisdom, you should also be careful not to condition your children for disaster by cutting them off from God or the blessings He can bring through a father figure in their life. Now, look at Joseph again; his brothers consistently attacked him out of jealousy because he was the star child. His heart was pure, and he resolved never to take anything from his father; in contrast, his brothers were stealing from their father, even though the flock was meant for them.

Listen closely; as I said, the distinction between star kids and others often comes down to their heart and spiritual inclinations; recognizing and nurturing these qualities in your children is paramount. This doesn't mean you need to start practicing favoritism in your home regarding your children, but about discerning and nurturing the unique gifts and callings God has placed in each child. In 1 Samuel 16:7, when Samuel was sent to anoint one of Jesse's sons as the future king of Israel, God reminded him, *"Look not on his countenance, or the height of his stature; because I have refused him: for the Lord seeth not as man seeth; for man looketh on the outward appearance, but the Lord looketh on the heart"* (KJV). This principle is fundamental when recognizing the star in your children. You must look beyond external factors and pay attention to your children's hearts and spiritual inclinations.

Recognizing The Star In Your Children Involves Several Key Aspects:

Spiritual Sensitivity: Pay attention to your child's spiritual inclinations; do they show an unusual interest in spiritual matters? Are they sensitive to God's voice even at a young age? Samuel's childhood calling (1 Samuel 3) is an excellent example.

Unique Gifts and Talents: Every child has gifts, but star children often display extraordinary abilities in certain areas. These could be intellectual, creative, leadership, or other gifts. Recognize and nurture these gifts.

Character and Integrity: Star children often display powerful character and integrity, as Joseph did, even in the face of temptation and adversity.

Visionary Thinking: Children with a unique calling will most likely have big dreams and visions for their future, much like Joseph with his dreams.

Resilience: Star children often face unusual challenges but display remarkable resilience. Think about David's courage against Goliath. He could see deeper than everyone else when he looked at that obstacle called Goliath.

Understanding your responsibility to your star child

What I need to note for you here is that these are things you should do for all your children because everyone is a start in their way. However, you should note those with unique callings and do what is needed.

Protection: As mentioned earlier, star children often face spiritual attacks, so as a parent, you must provide spiritual covering through prayer and godly upbringing. Psalm 127:3 reminds us, *"Lo, children are a heritage of the Lord: and the fruit of the womb is his reward"* (KJV).

Nurture: Recognizing potential is just the start. You must actively nurture your children's gifts and callings. Proverbs 22:6 says, *"Train up a child in the way he should go: and when he is old, he will not depart from it"* (KJV).

Balance: While recognizing every child's particular calling is essential, it's also important not to show favoritism or neglect other children. As I have said and repeated, "Each child is unique and valuable in God's eyes."

Preparation: Star children often face unique challenges in life, so you must prepare them spiritually, physically, and even emotionally for these challenges.

Humility: Help your star children understand that their gifts are from God and will be used for His glory, not self-exaltation. 1 Corinthians 4:7 asks, *"For who maketh thee to differ from another? And what hast thou that thou didst not receive? Now if thou didst receive it, why dost thou glory as if thou hadst not received it?"* (KJV).

In essence, recognizing the star in your children is about discerning and nurturing the unique gifts and callings that God has placed in them. It will demand spiritual sensitivity, careful observation, and intentional nurturing. By creating a godly environment through practices like the family altar, providing protection and guidance, and helping your children understand their gifts in the context of serving God and others, you are playing a role in helping your star children fulfill their God-given

destinies.

CHAPTER SEVEN

THE POWER OF YOUR FAMILY ALTAR

"Your family's destiny is fortified by the incense of prayer rising from your altar; never underestimate its power."

Shielding Your Family's Future And Destinies

Understanding The Right Family Dynamics

I n our walk with God, several sacred truths often get neglected by even the most devout believers sometimes, and one such truth, which I've come to understand deeply, is the significance of tithing. And when I talk about tithing, I don't want you to start overthinking; I know that there are several arguments in certain circles as to whether tithing is biblical or not, but what you should ask yourself is, "Do I have an obligation to give to the kingdom of God?", "Do I have an obligation to see the kingdom of God expand on the earth?" "Do I have a responsibility to see that God's intention on the earth is fulfilled?" When you can sincerely answer these questions, you will see that there is a demand of God upon your life; therefore, giving to the house of God can never be over-emphasized; in fact, you should start working towards going beyond 10% because if you have indeed given the Lord your life, then giving him any other thing should be pretty straightforward. These vital lessons, especially about tithing, were something I learned from my mother, a woman of unshakable faith and dedication to God. She often said, "When you eat your tithe, you steal from yourself." This simple yet powerful statement captures a fundamental spiritual principle many have failed to understand. Tithing is not merely about financial obligation; it's a spiritual covenant with far-reaching implications. As recorded in Malachi 3:8-9, *"Will a man rob God? Yet ye have robbed me. But ye say, wherein have we robbed thee? In tithes and offerings. Ye are cursed with a curse: for ye have robbed me, even this whole nation."* This verse reveals that withholding tithes is tantamount to robbing God, and the consequence is a curse.

My mother's devotion to God was absolute, a quality I pray your children will also attribute to you. Her commitment to spiritual principles set a powerful example that shaped my understanding of faith and family dynamics. Do you not know that your actions and words within the family unit have consequences? Especially in our children's spiritual and emotional development. Think about the impact of seemingly innocuous behaviors like gossiping or murmuring at home. These actions, which we often dismiss as harmless, will profoundly affect your children's character formation. Proverbs 26:20 says, *"Where no wood is, there the fire goeth out: so where there is no talebearer, the strife ceaseth."* When children are exposed to and adopt these negative behaviors, you inadvertently rob them of their dignity and integrity. Also, speaking ill of your spouse in front of children is a grievous error many parents commit.

This behavior sows seeds of discord that will have long-lasting effects on the family. This is why Ephesians 4:29 tells us, *"Let no corrupt communication proceed out of your mouth, but that which is good to the use of edifying, that it may minister grace unto the hearers."* By refraining from harmful speech about your spouse, you are also protecting your children from emotional turmoil and conflicting loyalties.

In essence, if, as a parent, you keep engaging in these destructive behaviors, they will create a conflict in your children's hearts; your children will find themselves torn between loyalty to both parents, feeling guilty each time they have to show love for daddy if they think they are supporting mommy; or feeling guilty for showing love to mommy when daddy was expecting them to pick his side and also hate mommy. This internal struggle will drive them to seek love and acceptance from strangers because they now feel unable to fully embrace the love of either parent without betraying the other. This is also a subtle form of emotional manipulation that will have devastating consequences on a child's ability to form healthy relationships in the future.

Why are all these important when talking about the family altar? You will never be able to raise a powerful and effective family altar if all these are not taken care of. You must teach your children spiritual laws and principles and create a healthy home of love and respect for both the husband and wife and even the children because, without them, there is no peace and emotional stability in our house.

Curses And Your Family Altar

Let us now look deeper into the issue of curses and their spiritual implications. In the spirit realm, contradictions can find resolution, and curses can be diluted. Although some curses may not even be broken from your entire family, they can be significantly weakened through your spiritual devotions. This is where your family altar is meant to serve as a powerful mechanism for keeping curses at bay, but when spirituality within the family begins to wane, it will weaken the altar. Curses will regain strength and recycle their negative influences on you and the family. You must know about your family altar and never forget that every act of pressing into God's presence through prayer, worship, and obedience is an investment in securing your family's future against curses, negativity, or demonic attacks. The incense that rises from your family altar and spiritual practices is a preemptive strike against potential disasters that have yet to manifest. Also, walking in rebellion against God's principles and your altar will activate those curses that couldn't take hold of you before, and soon, they will be able to dominate you.

When God first called Saul, he was a humble believer, almost fearful of his divine ordination. 1 Samuel 10:22 recounts, *"Therefore they enquired of the LORD further, if the man should yet come thither. And the LORD answered, Behold, he hid himself among the stuff."* This initial humility pleased God and strengthened his altar before the Lord. However, as time passed, pride began to take root in Saul's heart, leading him to believe he could serve God on his terms. This gradual departure from humble obedience to prideful self-reliance must become a cautionary tale for all believers. When you begin to think you can serve God in your way, disregarding His commands and the guidance of spiritual leaders and fathers he has placed over you, you inadvertently invite curses into your life and family. Saul's disobedience to his spiritual father, Samuel, escalated to the point where he threatened the person God had used to elevate him to kingship.

The story takes a dramatic turn when God instructs Samuel to anoint David as the new king. 1 Samuel 16:2 reveals Saul's fear: *"Samuel said, how can I go? If Saul hears it, he will kill me. And the LORD said, take a heifer with thee, and say, I come to sacrifice to the LORD."* This divine strategy of using sacrifice as a shield against Saul's wrath symbolizes the mystery that obedience and sacrifice can protect you in the face of opposition and spiritual warfare.

You may be under the influence of diluted curses passed down through generations without even realizing it (these curses are there because of your devotion and spiritual altar; they are weak and cannot manifest over you. Nevertheless, they are still there waiting for your rebellion against God and his principles to activate them). These spiritual impediments can manifest in various forms of struggle, failure, or persistent negative patterns in our lives and families. The question is, "Can we ever be truly free from these curses?" The answer is YES! But it requires decisive action and an unshakable commitment to spiritual principles.

When you depart this earthly life, you must ensure that you are not escaping responsibility but rather leaving a legacy of blessings for future generations. Before leaving this world, live a life that breaks every curse. The essence is so that your children can be free from them. Do not just think of diluting the curses so that it doesn't have dominion over you, but the moment you are going, your children will begin to suffer it. This is a selfish mindset, a mindset of King Hezekiah, who said, *"Good is the word of the LORD which thou hast spoken. He said moreover, For there shall be peace and truth in my days"* (Isaiah 39:8); why did he make this statement, it is because the prophet had just told him that because of his actions, there is curse and doom upon the land. Still, it will not be in his day; it would be in the days of his children; instead of praying to God and pleading for the curse to be lifted, he was happy, saying, "As long as the trouble will not come in my days, ten no big deal" What a disgrace for a parent! This is not a mindset any of us should emulate; our calling is to protect and bless the next generation, not merely secure our peace and wait for curses to reactivate in the days of our children.

The family altar is a powerful tool in bringing your family closer to God and combating these generational curses. While prayer can dilute curses, the ultimate goal should be their destruction through obedience and spiritual warfare because curses can be reversed through steadfast obedience to God's word and principles. Look at Deuteronomy 30:19: *"I call heaven and earth to record this day against you, that I have set before you life and death, blessing and cursing: therefore choose life, that both thou and thy seed may live."* Through the sacrifice of Christ, you have all it takes to get those curses out of your life, and as long as you stay with God, I assure you that you can obliterate them and ultimately see them destroyed out of your life. I mean completely.

The curse of idolatry is particularly insidious, and if not overwhelmed by God's blessings, it can revert to its concentrated form and defeat you. This spiritual explanation explains why many people even believe they keep experiencing cycles of victory followed by defeat. Do you know what? The key to breaking this cycle is consistent prayer, obedience, and a burning family altar that neutralizes concentrated curses.

Know this: every time you pray, you actively neutralize these concentrated curses in your family, allowing for continual spiritual ascension. The most effective strategy for sustained victory is to rise higher spiritually while lifting other family members alongside you. As you rise higher spiritually, you are accumulating spiritual blessings, and the accumulation of blessings creates a spiritual environment where curses find it increasingly difficult to work or regain their potency.

Strengthening Destines By The Mystery Of Altars

Also, the purpose of the family altar extends beyond neutralizing or destroying curses; it also strengthens destinies and reinforces God's ordained blessings for your family. This dual function of protection and empowerment is critical in securing a prosperous future for generations; hence, you must never joke about the potency and viability of your family altar.

The Passion Translation of Psalm 22:28-30 gives us a vivid picture of this spiritual reality by saying, *"For the Lord is King of all, taking charge of all the nations. Right now, while they're still eating their full at the feast, all the prosperous people of the earth will feast and worship. All those descended to the dust will kneel before Him, even those who can't keep themselves alive! His spiritual seed shall serve Him. Future generations will hear from us about the wonders of the Sovereign Lord."* This shows us that as you serve and worship God, you create a spiritual altar that will speak into the future. Your worship becomes a catalyst for deliverance and freedom for future generations. Your children can conquer the complications and struggles that took you years to overcome in a fraction of the time. This is why you often see your children achieving things beyond your reach, becoming more intelligent and more capable than you ever were. Nevertheless, this rapid advancement can sometimes lead to a sense of superiority in children, causing them to underestimate the struggles and sacrifices of their parents, so you must constantly remind them that their current vantage point is a result of the obstacles we parents have cleared from their path.

As you consistently serve and worship God, you'll notice a transformation not just in your own life but in the lives of your children, whether biological, adopted, or even spiritual children. Your business ventures will flourish, your dreams will materialize, and every aspect of your life will begin to shine with divine favor. This sudden brightness might seem surprising, but it results from someone moving spiritual clouds, breaking curses, and activating destinies through a mighty altar backed by fervent prayers and obedience.

This year, regardless of the strength or duration of past failures and disasters, I pray that you will witness a difference because of your commitment to the family altar in the mighty name of Jesus. The power of God will touch you, your children, your loved ones, and your entire family; areas that were once marked by struggle will now overflow with blessings in the mighty name of Jesus. And I pray that Isaiah 61:7 will become your testimony in the mighty name of Jesus. *"For your shame, ye shall have double; and for confusion, they shall rejoice in their portion: therefore in their land they shall possess the double: everlasting joy shall be unto them."*

Binding The Strong Man

Spiritual Warfare, Wealth, And The Battle For Your Soul

In spiritual warfare and the pursuit of wealth, you must realize that covenant people don't chase after money or material things; instead, these things pursue them. This is beautifully seen in Isaiah 60:5 (KJV), which says, *"Then thou shalt see, and flow together, and thine heart shall fear, and be enlarged; because the abundance of the sea shall be converted unto thee, the forces of the Gentiles shall come unto thee."* When the wealthy of the nations come to bow before you, they acknowledge a fundamental spiritual reality that true wealth originates from a divine source. As they prostrate themselves, faces to the dust in worship, they are partaking in a profoundly symbolic act. In the natural world, dust is often seen as something to be eliminated, wiped away from our possessions and living spaces. However, in the spiritual realm, dust carries a profound significance that we must understand to grasp the full implications of this act of worship. The Bible provides a fascinating perspective on dust in the context of spiritual blessings. Job 22:24 (KJV) says, *"Then shalt thou lay up gold as dust, and the gold of Ophir as the stones of the brooks."* This verse shows us that gold becomes as familiar as dust to those walking in covenant with God. In line with God's purposes, the family altar grants us access to the heavenly riches, allowing us to walk on the earth just as we will in holy places where the streets are paved with the purest gold (Revelation 21:21).

Isaiah 49:23 (KJV) further elaborates on this: *"And kings shall be thy nursing fathers, and their queens thy nursing mothers: they shall bow down to thee with their face toward the earth, and lick up the dust of thy feet, and thou shalt know that I am the LORD: for they shall not be ashamed that wait for me."* This clear picture of kings and queens bowing down and licking the dust at your feet is not about humiliation but recognizing the superior value of your spiritual wealth over earthly riches. In this divine economy, you become a commander of what the world's kings desperately seek. While they chase after earthly wealth, you walk in heavenly places where what we tread upon is the very substance they keep struggling to acquire. This elevated spiritual position is not achieved through human striving but through humble submission to God's will and the consistent practice of family altars.

For many people who keep becoming lost in the pursuit of wealth, I want you to know that there is a stark warning that is given in Mark 8:36 (KJV): *"For what shall it profit a man if he shall gain the whole world, and lose his soul?"* This verse reveals a dangerous transaction many unwittingly enter into, "they are trading their eternal soul for temporary earthly gain." When one trades their soul to the devil in exchange for material prosperity, they may indeed gain access to wealth on this earth, but at the cost of eternal damnation.

Don't forget, we earlier established that everyone is shaped by someone or something; this means that your maker determines your ultimate destination. If Satan is the one shaping your life and values, his address is Hell, or more permanently, the Lake of Fire will become your final destination. Remember Revelation 20:10 (KJV): *"And the devil that deceived them was cast into the lake of fire and brimstone, where the beast and the false prophet are, and shall be tormented day and night forever and ever."*

Do you keep seeing why the family altar is of paramount importance? When you bring your children to the family altar, you are not merely performing a religious ritual; you are connecting their souls to a holy order - the altar of God and this spiritual connection will serve as a powerful protection against the temptations and deceptions of the enemy. In the world today, we see sinners who appear to be stars - pseudo-stars shining with wealth and fame; and their apparent success often comes from trading their souls to Satan. This trend has become so prevalent that even unbelievers who do not yet submit to Christ are beginning to recognize and speak out against it, with many musicians refusing to go down that destructive path.

Well, just in case you have made this terrible bargain at any point in time, I want you to know that is hope. You can renounce that trade and reclaim your soul if you have breath. However, this process is not without its challenges because satan will not relinquish his claim easily, which is why you cannot undertake this battle alone. Reclaiming your soul and giving it back to God will require maintaining a solid spiritual defense, and this is where the family altar becomes indispensable. This will not just be your biological family altar. You will need the altar of a spiritual family, that is, your church and pastor, to back you up as you attempt to reclaim your soul and hand it over to God. If you go alone, you may become a casualty of spiritual warfare.

Jesus said in Mark 3:27 (KJV), *"No man can enter into a strong man's house, and spoil his goods, except he will first bind the strong man; and then he will spoil his house."* In this scripture, Satan is the strong man, and your soul is the precious good he seeks to keep, but who can bind this strong man? Only a more muscular man, and that is Jesus Christ Himself. He is the one who can bind the devil and deliver your soul from captivity. So submit to Christ and allow the church of Christ and a spiritual father's altar back your altar and your family altar. This way, you will experience victory and freedom from the enemy more efficiently.

Your family altar is meant to stand as a bulwark against the enemy's attempts to steal, kill, and destroy. It should be where heavenly wealth is accumulated, curses are broken, and souls are protected and reclaimed. Maintaining a solid family altar will secure your spiritual welfare and create a legacy of faith and prosperity for generations. Don't forget, the real wealth lies not in earthly possessions but in the richness of a soul fully surrendered to God and protected by His mighty hand.

CHAPTER EIGHT

WALKING IN COVENANT

"Success is not for your comfort alone; it is God's tool to showcase His power in your life."

Your Success Is God's Advertisement

Because of God's covenant on your life, God intends that your success serves as God's tool to advertise Himself, and what this means is that if your light does not shine, how will the world glorify your Father in Heaven? If you are living below your potential and constantly finding excuses, the world will not glorify Him through you. But then, when your light begins to shine, you attract attention. I have often said this again and again, "Satan is not a competition for God; the real struggle is between two forces, and that is God and mammon, God and money."

You need to start knowing that money is a spirit and will cause good people, even those without principles, to do foolish things. This is precisely why God wants you to have it. The silver and gold belong to Him. If you are wise, you will realize that we do not have much time on this earth; everything is concluding and wrapping up. This means that God is in a hurry to pour out His greatness upon His people, advertise Himself, and use the greatness of your life to bring sinners into the kingdom.

Now, when you look at Isaiah 5, you will hear God lamenting, and I can listen to that same lament over the body of Christ even today. His heart cries, *"My well-beloved had a vineyard in a very fruitful field..."* (Isaiah 5:1, KJV). He said He plowed it, removed the stones, and planted it with the best vines. The Church of Jesus Christ has been given the best. And after salvation, what we have are faithful men of God. We can see things before they happen; more often than not, we know why things happen the way they do! Now, whenever the Lord shows me things to be revealed, I do not hold back from telling these things. I have stood in the gap for the land, the body of Christ, and even for America. Even during the COVID-19 crisis in America, I obeyed God throughout. This is one of the reasons why God fights for me, even in my weakest moments; if you try to fight me, you are fighting God, and you may not live to tell the story. That is the truth.

There are several people I cover as a spiritual father whose lives would be much better, but their biggest enemy is themselves. I can pray and fast for you, but then you can also turn around and gossip about me, talking about me behind my back. What you do not even realize is that most of the time, whatever you accuse me of, maybe not even one percent of it is true. And yet, you can be out there doing foolish things by speaking about me. I am not just speaking for myself; I am speaking for spiritual fathers and Christian fathers who have labored so much, yet the younger generation, instead of submitting to learn wisdom and excel, thinks it is better to gossip, criticize, and ridicule them. You need to be careful and examine yourself.

Before you talk about people, it's best that you check your own life. We are all standing and speaking by God's grace and mercy. And by His mercy, I run with His purpose.

Look at Moses and the Israelites; everyone was in captivity, including those who gossiped about him. Why did God not use them to free the people if they were so great? Why did God wait 30 years? If they were that important, why did He not raise them in Egypt to free the people? No, God had to pray for Moses to step into his calling. He went to Moses, negotiated with him, and waited because God's name was on the line. He could have rushed things, but He would rather wait and have the right person do the job. This is how important fathers are, and you must take them seriously!

Now, let's go back to God's tool for advertisement because if you joke with this, you are essentially taking God's covenant and desires upon your life without seriousness.

Matthew 5:16 (KJV) says, *"Let your light shine before men, that they may see your good works, and glorify your Father which is in heaven."* This encapsulates what it means for your success to be a testament to God's greatness. You are not just advancing your interests when you excel in your endeavors, rise above mediocrity, and achieve impossible things. Still, you are showcasing God's power and favor in your life. Think of Joseph in Genesis. His rise from an enslaved person to the second-in-command of Egypt was not just for his benefit; it was God's way of positioning him to save many lives and bring glory to His name. Genesis 41:39-40 (KJV) says, *"And Pharaoh said unto Joseph, Forasmuch as God hath showed thee all this, there is none so discreet and wise as thou art: Thou shalt be over my house, and according unto thy word shall all my people be ruled: only in the throne will I be greater than thou."* Do you see Joseph's success directly resulted from God's favor and was a powerful testimony to Pharaoh and all of Egypt?

Also, when the Lord blesses and lifts you in success, it is not merely for your enjoyment or comfort. It is a tool in God's hands to draw others to Himself because your prosperity and lifting are meant to be a beacon of hope for those around you and tangible evidence of God's faithfulness and power. As you employ people, invest in businesses, and expand your influence, you create opportunities for others to see God's goodness in action.

Nevertheless, it is essential to understand that this success comes with a responsibility. Deuteronomy 8:18 (KJV) says, *"But thou shalt remember the LORD thy God: for it is he that giveth thee power to get wealth, that he may establish his covenant which he sware unto thy fathers, as it is this day."* The ability to generate wealth and achieve success is a gift from God, given to us so that we can establish His covenant on the earth.

The Dangers Of Rebelling Against Spiritual Fathers

Rebellion Is A Deadly Trap

You should know now that rebellion is never a trivial matter; it is a deadly trap that can lead to unimaginable consequences. When you rebel against a spiritual father, you are not just rejecting a man; you are rejecting a divine covering and a blessing that God has placed over your life for protection, sustenance, and growth. Suppose your spiritual father, a wellspring of living water, imparts that same water to you by the laying on of hands. I want you to know that you can go out and dig a well, but you need to understand that your well is sustained not by your efforts but by your father's spiritual impartation. This means the well is not what gives you water. Instead, it is you who provides water to the well. The fantastic part is that they will fail when others come and try to take that well from you. Why? Because the source of your well is not in the physical realm, it is sustained by the spiritual water imparted to you by your father. This is why those who opposed Isaac in Genesis 26:12-15 had to stop trying to steal his wells eventually. The Philistines could fill his wells with dirt but could not take God's blessing upon them through his Father Abraham. No matter how hard they tried, the water did not flow for them because the blessing was not theirs.

Isaac didn't depend on the well for his sustenance; the well depended on him. Do you see the pattern? Your career, your business, your calling, they all rely on the anointing you carry, which is often passed down through your spiritual father; as a child of God, you should know that it is not the work of your hands that keeps things moving; it's the spiritual blessings upon your life that sustains it all. But when you rebel against that spiritual father, you are cutting yourself off from that flow and becoming like those who tried to steal Isaac's water, only to end up with dust.

Rebellion is a subtle trap; at first, it will even look like an act of independence and as though you are breaking free from a limitation, but do you know what? In reality, it is the very thing that will lead you to bondage because rebellion turns wells of blessing into dry pits of serpents and bondage. The Bible says in Proverbs 17:11 (KJV), *"An evil man seeketh only rebellion: therefore a cruel messenger shall be sent against him."* That cruel messenger is the consequence of your rebellion, the spiritual drought that follows, the confusion, the chaos, and the scars left behind when you walk out from under the covering God placed over you.

I want you to imagine a young man who thinks he is strong enough to take on the world alone and then rebels against his spiritual father, considering he no longer needs that guidance. What will happen is that at first, life will look as though he's doing fine, but this is just the devil deceiving him so that he can entirely be trapped; so it will look as though his well is still producing water, his career is thriving, and his relationships are still intact, but slowly, things will start to dry up. The favor that once surrounded him will fade, and the once-open doors will begin to close. What happened? He cut himself off from the source of his blessing, so the well that was once overflowing with life is now a pit of dirt, shame, and regret. In Numbers 12, we see a striking example of rebellion when Miriam and Aaron spoke against Moses; they questioned his authority, asking, *"Hath* the Lord indeed spoken only by Moses? hath he not spoken also by us?" (Numbers 12:2, KJV). They rebelled against the spiritual authority God had placed over them. And what happened? Miriam was struck with leprosy, a physical manifestation of the spiritual disease that had already taken root in her heart. Her rebellion cost her dearly, just as rebellion always does.

I also want you to understand that rebellion doesn't just happen overnight; it starts as a seed and a small thought, "I don't need this covering. I can make it on my own." That seed grows, and before you know it, you are walking out from under the very protection God placed over your life. You have let pride take the place of submission, and that pride leads you down a path of destruction. Isaiah 30:1 (KJV) says, "*Woe to the rebellious children, saith the Lord, that take counsel, but not of me; and that cover with a covering, but not of my spirit, that they may add sin to sin.*" God's warning is clear: "Rebellion leads to sin, and sin leads to destruction."

Rebellion

Breach Of Covenant

In your spiritual walk, you must understand that your relationship with spiritual fathers is not just a mentorship; it is a covenant, and a covenant is a sacred agreement, one that is bound by spiritual laws and principles. When you rebel against a spiritual father, you are breaking that covenant, and the thing about covenants is that they carry both blessings and curses. When you honor the covenant, the blessings flow, but when you break it, the consequences will follow. Look at Malachi 4:5-6 (KJV): "*Behold, I will send you Elijah the prophet before the coming of the great and dreadful day of the Lord: And he shall turn the heart of the fathers to the children, and the heart of the children to their fathers, lest I come and smite the earth with a curse.*" This scripture clarifies that there is a divine connection between fathers and children, a connection that, when broken, leads to a curse. Rebellion is a breach of that heavenly order.

Just as Elisha received a double portion of Elijah's spirit because he honored his spiritual father (2 Kings 2:9-10, KJV), so do we receive a double portion of the blessings and favor when we celebrate the spiritual fathers God placed over us. But when you rebel, you are cutting yourself off from that inheritance. It's like the prodigal son in Luke 15, who demanded his inheritance and left his father's house in rebellion. He thought he could make it on his own, but he ended up in a hovel, scarred and broken by his rebellion. You see, What the prodigal son didn't understand is that his blessing wasn't just in the wealth he received; it was in the covering and wisdom of his father. When he left that covering, he lost everything. His rebellion cost him dearly, and though he was eventually restored, the scars of his rebellion remained.

But despite all the dangers of rebellion, there is still a path to restoration; just like the prodigal son, you can return to the Father's house. God is merciful, and He is always ready to forgive. 1 John 1:9 (KJV) reminds us, "*If we confess our sins, he is faithful and just to forgive us our sins, and to cleanse us from all unrighteousness.*" But repentance is not just about saying sorry; it's about a complete change of heart and a total surrender to God's order by seeing genuine forgiveness from the father you rebelled against. True repentance means that you must recognize the error of your ways and fall back into alignment with God's spiritual authority over your life. You must submit to the covering of your spiritual father so that the blessing can flow back into your life. The scars of rebellion may remain, but they will only serve as reminders of the consequences of stepping out of God's will. Isaiah 1:19 (KJV) says, "*If ye be willing and obedient, ye shall eat the good of the land.*" *Obedience restores what rebellion has stolen. It opens the floodgates of blessing*

Unlocking The Fullness Of Life

Through Spiritual Guidance

Look at 2 Timothy 2:1-7 (TPT), where the apostle Paul addresses his spiritual son Timothy; Paul said, *"Timothy, my dear son, live your life empowered by God's free-flowing grace, which is your true strength. There is grace in reading, found in the anointing of Jesus and your union with Him."* In this verse of the Bible, we have a powerful example of what it means to be a spiritual son mirrored in the relationship between Paul and Timothy; this is truly a blueprint for all spiritual sons who seek to learn from their fathers.

From their relationship, you should see that the evidence of true sonship lies in your ability to learn from your spiritual father. Paul doesn't just suggest learning; he commands it. If you cannot humble yourself and truly learn from your father, you are setting yourself up for failure in life and destiny. Non-learners often find themselves caught in the trap of repeated failure because without learning, you are doomed to repeat the same mistakes until you are destroyed. A life devoid of learning is a life devoid of progress. When you fail to learn, you will become a perpetual loser, lacking the insight and wisdom that only comes through genuine submission to the tutelage of your spiritual father.

Let me paint a picture for you here; I want you to imagine someone who keeps making the same poor decisions, perhaps drinking and driving and repeatedly landing in trouble. Such a person may have had numerous opportunities to learn from their mistakes, but they will continue to make the same blunder repeatedly because they are not learners. This is how non-learners always remain stuck in cycles of destruction, all because they fail to pick lessons from their experiences or the wisdom of others. Now, don't deceive yourself into thinking that just because you are covered by grace, you can ignore the instructions of your spiritual father. The grace that sustains you in your journey flows from the divine wisdom imparted to you through your spiritual father. When you neglect the lessons he offers, you are cutting yourself off from that grace, and when you go against his instructions, you are setting yourself up for destruction. As a spiritual son or daughter, you must always humble yourself and recognize the treasure in the lessons your father imparts.

The Power Of Transferring Knowledge

Paul tells Timothy, *"Deposit into faithful leaders who are competent to teach the congregation the same revelations."* The ability to transfer what you have learned to others is a mark of true spiritual maturity. This is not merely acquiring knowledge but about carrying the wisdom and anointing passed down from your spiritual father and imparting it to the next generation; this is to let you know that true sons are conduits of revelation because they can absorb what is taught and pass it on faithfully from their fathers to the sons that God will bring towards them.

Have you not noticed that some people may not have the most visible or extraordinary potential in life, but because they are learners, they often surpass those who seem more naturally gifted? I am saying that a star that doesn't know how to shine is useless, no matter how bright you may be in theory. Your ability to shine both in the day and the dark depends on how well you have learned from those before you.

I still remember an instance in my own life when my father was preaching, and I was distracted. That day, I had a significant business deal that required my attention, but as I reached for my phone, the Lord spoke to me and said, "Your father is on the pulpit." At that moment, I realized that no trade, no deal, and no financial gain could compare to the blessing of honoring my father as he ministered. That realization was a turning point for me and a reminder that the blessings we seek are often tied not to our efforts but to the honor we show to our fathers. Sadly, many people are missing out on the revelations and blessings God has for them because they are distracted. Whether you're texting, scrolling through social media, or just mentally absent, when your father is present, you're allowing these distractions to rob you of the impartation God wants to give you through your father. "Learning requires focus & being present spiritually, emotionally, and physically so that you can capture the full weight of what is being imparted."

The Trap of Thinking You Know It All

One of the most significant barriers to learning is the belief that you already know everything; this is because when your heart becomes closed, thinking you have learned all there is to see, you prevent yourself from receiving new insights and revelations. This is a form of pride that can be spiritually deadly. Unlearning is just as crucial as learning because, without discarding outdated knowledge, you can never make room for new revelations. Do you remember Peter in John 13:8. When Jesus began washing the disciples' feet, Peter initially refused, saying, "You shall never wash my feet!" But Jesus responded, "If I do not wash you, you have no part with me." Peter thought he knew what was right, but in his ignorance, he nearly cut himself off from the blessings that Jesus was imparting through the simple act of foot washing. You see, learning requires humility, and so Peter had to humble himself to receive the impartation of honor, dignity, and authority that came with the washing of his feet.

The lesson here is profound: You must never allow your preconceived notions to block your ability to receive from your spiritual father because there are dimensions of spiritual truth and authority you cannot access until you humble yourself enough to receive them. More often than not, the most striking revelations come when you are willing to let go of what you think you know and allow yourself to be taught anew.

Playing By The Rules To Receive The Crown

Paul continued in 2 Timothy by metaphorizing an athlete

competing in a race. He said, *"If anyone competes as an athlete, he does not receive the victor's crown unless he competes according to the rules."* Just as an athlete must follow the rules to win the race, so must we follow the divine principles laid out for us by God through our spiritual fathers. Ignorance of these rules will not exempt you from disqualification. Breaking the rules, even if you are the fastest runner, will lead to defeat. Now imagine a sprinter who crosses into another runner's lane while he is running. Do you realize that even if he finishes first and may even break a record, he will be disqualified because he broke the rules?

In the same way, it is not enough to be gifted or anointed; if you do not follow the spiritual principles your Father has imparted, you risk disqualifying yourself from the blessings and rewards God has for you. To receive the victor's crown in life, you must first learn the rules, and those rules are often imparted through your spiritual father. Your father knows the path; he has walked it before you, and to assume that you can go through life without his guidance is to walk unthinkingly into traps and pitfalls that could have easily been avoided if only you had humbled yourself to learn.

Returning to the story of Peter and Jesus, we see that washing feet was not just a physical act but a spiritual impartation of life. Jesus told Peter, *"If I don't wash you, you have no part with me."* Though seemingly simple, foot washing was a conduit for spiritual authority, dignity, and life. In the same way, learning from your spiritual father is not just about acquiring knowledge; it is about receiving life. You may be too hurried to receive the anointing; you may rush through spiritual lessons, distracted by the cares of life, not realizing that the very impartation you are neglecting could be the key to your breakthrough. The distractions you allow to interfere with your learning deprive you of the life God wants to impart through your father. I pray that your spirit will catch this.

The life that comes through learning is not something you can obtain through your efforts alone. It is a spiritual impartation that can only be received through humility and submission to God's authority over you. The battles you face, whether internal or external, can often be won simply by receiving your father's impartation of wisdom and authority. But if you are distracted or too prideful to learn, you will miss out on something that could change your life.

But then again, it's never too late to humble yourself and begin learning. No matter how far you may have strayed or how many mistakes you may have made, God is always ready to restore you when you come back under the cover of your spiritual father.

The necessity of genuinely humbling yourself to learn from a Father cannot be overstated. Your spiritual growth, success, and ability to walk in the fullness of God's blessings all hinge on your willingness to submit to the authority of your spiritual father and learn from him. When you can humble yourself to know, you are opening the door to revelation, wisdom, and impartations that will sustain you and elevate you to new dimensions of glory.

Let us, therefore, be diligent learners, always ready to receive the wisdom and guidance that God has placed in our lives through our spiritual fathers.

CHAPTER NINE

THE SACRED BURDEN OF LEADING

"The path to wisdom is paved with the humility to listen and learn from those who guide us."

The Power To Destroy Or Make

When Jesus looked at Judas Iscariot, His beloved disciple, and said, *"It would have been better for you not to have been born" (Matthew 26:24)*, He didn't just utter a simple statement. He revealed the depth of the consequences of betrayal and the gravity of our choices when we belittle our spiritual fathers. There is a profound truth in this moment that can be seen throughout life. The weight of our actions is often felt in eternity, which bears down upon those called to lead. Just as Paul warned us about the dangers of anger and how it can open the door to devastation, spiritual fathers must be aware that their emotions, words, and actions hold great power over the lives of those they are entrusted to guide.

Look at Moses, a man who experienced the burning bush, stood before the Shekinah glory, and survived the unspeakable presence of the Almighty on Mount Sinai. He carried a burden that few can understand, yet amid his journey, even Moses, the man closest to God, faced a moment of overwhelming frustration. In that moment, He cried out to God, not just as a "man of God," but as a man weary of the people he had been sent to lead. *"These people don't understand,"* Moses lamented, *"They don't know the fire I encountered; they don't see the weight of what I've been through with You, Lord."* In his frustration, Moses, chosen by God, called for a judgment to show them the seriousness of their actions. He said, *"If these people die the common death of men, then I am not sent by God."* He didn't stop there; he called upon God to create a new kind of death, one that would serve as an undeniable sign of their provocation. (Numbers 16:28-30)

And what happened next? The ground opened beneath them, swallowing them alive; wow, can you imagine that? It didn't just swallow them; it also swallowed all their families, homes, and everything they possessed. The earth became their grave. This wasn't just a show of divine power; it was a reminder of the responsibility that comes with being in a position of leadership, especially spiritual fatherhood. Moses' frustration led to a reckoning, and the weight of his anger, even justified as it may have been, altered the destinies of countless people. The anger of a spiritual father, a leader, carries more weight than most realize, and the consequences can be devastating. So, as a spiritual father, you should be careful; as a spiritual son, you must also be more cautious and respectful when approaching your father.

Fatherlessness Is The Source Of Broken Destinies

We live in a world where fatherlessness is a crisis, not just physically but spiritually. Just look around you, and you will see that most of the boys and girls in juvenile detention centers come from homes without fathers. In fact, over Seventy percent of teenagers who commit serious crimes come from the same kind of homes. Honestly speaking, the absence of a father figure, whether biological or spiritual, creates dangerous gaps in the lives of young people, and these gaps soon become chasms that lead to destruction, confusion, and chaos. In our world and the lives of so many people. I tell you the truth: a father's presence is not just needed; it is essential for shaping destinies.

To those God is raising as spiritual fathers, I say this: as much as you can, please, for mercy's sake, let's try and control our emotions. One of the greatest gifts that God has given me is the ability to control my feelings and anger but not let it dictate my actions. You see, there's power in your words and your reactions. You can either curse or bless, but each time you alter your words, their impact will always be seen in the lives of those under you. Let's look at Elisha, who, in a moment of anger, cursed Gehazi with leprosy; what if Elisha had taken the time to sit Gehazi down, to teach him the seriousness of the mission, to remind him that they were not hirelings, not men seeking material gain, but men of God with a purpose? The outcome could have been different; Gehazi's destiny might not have been shame and sickness.

This is not a caution to spiritual fathers; this is a caution to every one of you who may want to take your spiritual fathers for granted. You are playing a dangerous game and can be destroyed by it.

Seeing Beyond The Moment

We live in a chaotic world, and spiritual fathers are needed more than ever. I am talking about men and women who can see beyond the surface and discern the more profound spiritual realities at play. There are times in ministry when the revelations don't come at the beginning but in the middle or even at the end. Sometimes, after a service, everything floods in, and I receive insights about the people, the spiritual battles, and hidden truths in the spirit realm. If I were to document every revelation that comes to me in ministry, I am sure that the world itself wouldn't be able to contain the books. This is the reality of spiritual leadership; there's always more beneath the surface than people can see.

But this discernment doesn't just apply to great spiritual revelations but to the day-to-day moments of leadership, where spiritual fathers are called to guide their children away from disaster. I remember speaking with one of my spiritual children, warning them of a decision that could have destroyed their life. They were on the verge of making the worst mistake, thinking they could reverse it or manipulate the outcome. I told them plainly, "This is the worst mistake you're about to make." They didn't believe me initially, but I reassured them that no stubbornness or intimidation could move me from the truth. My anointing is raw; it's pure and cannot be purchased. You cannot buy me; no one can. I've prophesied to governors and men of power and stood my ground even when they thought they could use their position or influence to sway me. It's not possible. I once warned a governor, a man surrounded by corruption, that he would lose his election because of the blood on his hands; he didn't listen; instead, he trusted in his occultic politicians rather than a spiritual father, and when the time came, he lost precisely as I had prophesied. It wasn't about proving my gift; it was about the weight of consequences that come with turning away from God's path.

I have always clarified that my anointing and spiritual guidance cannot be bought. I have never accepted money for prophesying and never asked for anything in return for giving spiritual direction. Honestly, you cannot buy the blessings of God's hand. You cannot manipulate spiritual authority as far as I am concerned because my integrity cannot be compromised, and this is something I teach all who come under my leadership. You cannot lead effectively if you are not invested and not personally aligned with the vision God has given you. I said all this to show you that spiritual fatherhood is not a transactional relationship but a sacred commitment rooted in faith, integrity, and the pursuit of God's truth.

Far too many young preachers today think they know everything, so they rush into ministry without understanding the gravity of what they are stepping into. I often tell them that ministry is not a game nor a stage for your glory. Many of them are in a hurry to become spiritual fathers, and they do not realize that the role of a spiritual father is to stay vigilant, remain humble, and be open to God's direction. I can assure you that this sacrifice is not something many of these young ministers are ready for. I have only been able to come this far because I value spiritual instructions and counsel, but the consequences are grave for those who reject spiritual counsel.

Beloved, you may be a Spiritual father, or you may just be a spiritual son for now, or better still, you may be in both categories and by this, I mean that you may have a spiritual father guiding you and at the same time you may have sons in the Lord. Nevertheless, we must all come to the point where we realize that "Spiritual fatherhood" is not a light responsibility; it is a sacred burden where the lives and destinies of those you are called to lead rest in your hands. You must carry this weight with the utmost seriousness, understanding that every decision and every word you speak can shape or destroy those lives. Ultimately, the reward is not in the accolades or material blessings but in knowing that you have faithfully carried out the role God has given you, that you have nurtured lives, built destinies, and led with integrity.

God bless you!

CONCLUSION

We must be relentless in our pursuit of destiny, and valuing your spiritual father is one primary way to ensure you stay on course. As you must have now realized, spiritual fathers are not merely mentors or guides; they are divinely appointed vessels through which God's grace, wisdom, and protection flow. In the same way that a father cares for his child, a spiritual father watches over the spiritual growth, preservation, and success of those entrusted to him because God has promised never to leave or forsake us (Hebrews 13:5 KJV). One of the ways He keeps that promise is through the spiritual fathers He places in our lives. No matter what you do in life, you must never trivialize the necessity of staying deeply connected to your spiritual father because your destiny and fulfillment are directly tied to it.

The pathway to fulfilling God's will for your life is filled with challenges, trials, and tribulations, but God's protection and the guidance of a spiritual father will make the journey less treacherous. Our world is filled with opposition from spiritual forces, physical enemies, and even worldly systems. Yet, the presence and covering of your spiritual father can ensure that no competition or obstacle can stand against you.

Just look around you, and you will realize that the enemy's tactics have become more sophisticated; witchcraft has evolved, merging traditional spiritualities with technology, and this means that we are no longer fighting against the simple schemes of darkness; we are now facing a form of spiritual warfare that has become deeply intertwined with technological manipulation. This requires an even greater level of spiritual protection and discernment. Ephesians 6:12 (KJV) tells us, *"For we wrestle not against flesh and blood, but against principalities, against powers, against the rulers of the darkness of this world, against spiritual wickedness in high places."* The fight is no longer just against the familiar but against forces that have adapted to the technological age, weaponizing it to manipulate destinies and disrupt divine paths.

Thus, staying hooked on your spiritual father becomes even more imperative. When God gives you a father in the Lord, He has provided you with a shield, a guide, and a source of divine protection. The relationship between a spiritual father and his spiritual child is sacred and cannot be taken lightly. When you honor that relationship and submit to the instruction and correction of your spiritual father, you will be able to align yourself with divine order, bringing about spiritual covering and preservation.

Think about the relationship between Moses and Joshua; it is a prime example of the power that comes from staying connected to your spiritual father. In Joshua 1:5-8 (KJV), God spoke directly to Joshua and encouraged them to succeed. But what was the key that God gave Joshua? The key to his prosperity and success was adhering to the book of the law, which Moses, his spiritual father, gave him. Moses passed on divine instruction and wisdom, and Joshua's success depended on his faithfulness to what Moses had taught him. *"There shall not any man be able to stand before thee all the days of thy life: as I was with Moses, so I will be with thee: I will not fail thee, nor forsake thee."* (Joshua 1:5 KJV). This promise of God's continual presence and support came to Joshua not because he was a great warrior but because he was obedient to his spiritual father, followed his instructions, and meditated on them day and night. As a result, he experienced success.

Similarly, in today's spiritual walk, the wisdom and counsel of your spiritual father are the building blocks of your prosperity and destiny; the book of the law that Moses gave to Joshua symbolizes the divine teachings and instructions passed from spiritual fathers to their children so when you stay connected to your spiritual father and heed his words, you are also positioning yourself for success that the world cannot give and cannot take away.

A true spiritual father does not manipulate or deceive; he operates in the truth of God's word and leads with integrity. In our ministry, we hold fast to a standing law that any pastor who manipulates or tricks people to conduct ministry will face the consequences and become cursed. Do you know why? We know God is more than enough, and His truth sustains us. I mean, faithful ministry is not done through manipulation but by raising men and women who will live according to God's principles. Sadly, some leaders have fallen into the trap of using tricks and manipulation to extract money and gain influence. However, those genuinely called to be spiritual fathers must be above such things. We don't raise money; we raise men! And if the men we raise are raised well, they will naturally provide the resources needed to sustain the ministry. It's never about the money; it's about the people.

A spiritual father's words carry weight, and his prophecies can shape the destiny of his spiritual children. The Bible tells us of Jacob, who received the blessing of his father, Isaac. That blessing became the force that guided Jacob's steps and ordered his life. Genesis 28:12-13 (KJV) says, *"And he dreamed, and behold a ladder set up on the earth, and the top of it reached heaven: and behold the angels of God ascending and descending on it. And, behold, the Lord stood above it, and said, I am the Lord God of Abraham thy father, and the God of Isaac."* Jacob was connected to his father's blessing, which opened heaven to him. This is the power of staying hooked on your spiritual father. Just as Jacob didn't know that his journey would lead him to the same place where his grandfather Abraham had raised an altar, you too may not fully understand the depth of what your spiritual father's covering can do for you. Still, the blessings that flow from him will create pathways for your success and divine encounters.

The connection is spiritual and must not be taken lightly.

You have learned so much; the Lord has opened your eyes to this spiritual law. It's time to take action and become accountable to a spiritual father.

Do you want to see an increase and growth in your life?

You Know what to Do!

God bless you!

DAVID PHILEMON

A SPECIAL CALL TO SALVATION & NEW BEGINNINGS FROM APOSTLE DR. DAVID PHILEMON

Dear Beloved,
God loves you deeply and has brought you to this moment for a reason. No matter your past, His love and forgiveness are available to you.

The Bible says in John 3:16, "For God so loved the world that He gave His one and only Son, that whoever believes in Him shall not perish but have eternal life." Jesus Christ came to save you, offering you a new life of purpose and peace.

If you're ready to accept Jesus as your Lord and Savior, pray this simple prayer:

The Salvation Prayer

"Heavenly Father, I come to You in the Name of Jesus. I acknowledge that I am a sinner in need of a Savior. I believe that

Jesus Christ is Your Son, that He died for my sins, and that You raised Him from the dead. I repent of my sins and turn to You with my

Whole heart. Jesus, I ask You to come into my life. Be my Lord and my Savior. I surrender my life to You. Fill me with Your Holy Spirit, guide me on the path of righteousness, and help me to follow Your script for my life. Thank you, Father, for saving me. In the name of Jesus. Amen."

Welcome to the Family of God!

If you have just prayed this prayer, Congratulations! You are now a child of God, and heaven is rejoicing. Your journey has begun, and we're here to support you as you grow in faith and discover God's unique plans for you.

Next Steps:

• Connect with a Bible-believing church.

• Read the Bible Daily: God's Word is your guide.

• Pray Regularly: Prayer is your lifeline to God.

• Share Your Faith: Don't keep the good news to yourself.

ABOUT THE BOOK

"Riding on the Wings of a Father" is more than just a book; it's a blueprint for destiny. You will be set for a life of ease and obedience as you read. This is a journey of great transformation and exponential results.

Don't waste your time struggling in isolation, trying to figure out life on your own. Instead, embrace the principle of spiritual fatherhood. Submit, learn, and grow under the guidance of the one God has placed over your life. As you do, you will find that the path of destiny becomes more apparent, the burdens lighter, and your flight swifter. God has destined you to soar, so don't miss the opportunity to fly by neglecting the divine principle of spiritual fatherhood.